Better Homes and Gardens®

Holiday Crafts
KIDS CAN MAKE

© Copyright 1987 by Meredith Corporation, Des Moines, Iowa.
All Rights Reserved. Printed in the United States of America.
First Edition. Printing Number and Year: 15 14 13 12 11   96 95 94 93
Library of Congress Catalog Card Number: 86-62171
ISBN: 0-696-01605-2 (hard cover)
ISBN: 0-696-01606-0 (trade paperback)

BETTER HOMES AND GARDENS® BOOKS

Editor: Gerald M. Knox
Art Director: Ernest Shelton
Managing Editor: David A. Kirchner
Editorial Project Managers: James D. Blume, Marsha Jahns,
  Rosanne Mattson, Mary Helen Schiltz,

Crafts Editor: Joan Cravens
Senior Crafts Editors: Beverly Rivers, Sara Jane Treinen
Associate Crafts Editor: Elizabeth Porter

Associate Art Directors: Linda Ford Vermie, Neoma Alt West
  Randall Yontz
Assistant Art Directors: Lynda Haupert, Harijs Priekulis,
  Tom Wegner
Senior Graphic Designer: Darla Whipple-Frain
Graphic Designers: Mike Burns, Brian Wignall
Art Production: Director, John Berg; Associate, Joe Heuer;
  Office Manager, Emma Rediger

President, Book Group: Fred Stines
Vice President, General Manager: Jeramy Lanigan
Vice President, Retail Marketing: Jamie Martin
Vice President, Administrative Services: Rick Rundall

BETTER HOMES AND GARDENS® MAGAZINE
President, Magazine Group: James A. Autry
Vice President, Editorial Director: Doris Eby
Executive Director, Editorial Services: Duane L. Gregg

MEREDITH CORPORATE OFFICERS
Chairman of the Board: E. T. Meredith III
President: Robert A. Burnett
Executive Vice President: Jack D. Rehm

HOLIDAY CRAFTS KIDS CAN MAKE
Crafts Editor: Beverly Rivers
Editorial Project Manager: Mary Helen Schiltz
Graphic Designer: Darla Whipple-Frain
Electronic Text Processor: Cindy McClanahan

On the cover: See pages 14-19, 34-35, and 146-149.

Making decorations and
gifts is one way kids and grown-ups
celebrate the holidays throughout the year.
HOLIDAY CRAFTS KIDS CAN MAKE is full of ideas
just for *you* to create—for Valentine's Day,
for Christmas, and for every special day in between.

CONTENTS

TRIMS FROM FOOD
FOR THE
HOLIDAYS

You'll be surprised at the kinds of things you
can make with the supplies in your kitchen.
Use ordinary dry beans to make super
wreaths—one that's big enough to hang on
the front door or smaller ones that are just
the right size for the Christmas tree.
And when you mix ground cinnamon with
glue, you can make clay for ornaments that'll
always smell like something's baking.
Best of all, the projects are made in such
a way that they'll last for many years.

WREATHS

The next time your family goes to the grocery store, tag along and pick up an assortment of dry beans. Everyone will be delighted when they see what you can make from such a common kitchen food. Here are other supplies you will need to craft this country wreath.

GETTING STARTED

☐ Assorted beans
☐ Cinnamon sticks
☐ Whole cloves
☐ Mod Podge
☐ White crafts glue
☐ Florist's tape
☐ Plastic foam wreath

☐ Cardboard
☐ Chenille florist's stems
☐ Gathered trim
☐ Awl or pick
☐ 1 yard of ribbon
☐ Straight pins
☐ Scissors

1 DOING THE PROJECT

Use dry beans, corn, peas, barley, or any dry item similar to these. Pick beans with pretty colors. Put them all together in a large container and mix them with your hands.

2

Use plastic foam rings from the crafts stores for bean wreaths. Or, cut out small cardboard circles for smaller wreath ornaments. Use a compass to draw a 4-inch circle. Draw the center circle 1 inch or slightly more inside the other circle.

3 Wrap the plastic foam or cardboard circle with florist's tape from a flower shop or crafts store. Pull slightly on the tape while you are wrapping it around the wreath. Stretching the tape will cause it to stick to itself.

4 Use a pick or awl to poke two holes, side by side and 1 inch apart, completely through the wreath. (See the photograph, *above*.) Push one end of the chenille stem through each hole. Pull the stem ends far enough through the holes to twist them tightly together. The part that is not pulled through will make a loop on the back for hanging. Poke holes on the inside.

5 You are now ready to decorate the wreath. Glue the ruffle on first. Place a line of glue along the edge of the ring. Use your fingers to lay the ruffle in place. Stick the end of a straight pin into the fabric and foam to hold the ruffle in place until the glue is dry.

6 In a small bowl, mix one cup of beans with six heaping tablespoons of Mod Podge, available at a crafts store. The beans are white now, but they will dry clear and shiny. Place the ring over the bottom of a plastic bowl.

7 Spoon the mixture around the inside of the wreath. Cover the inside edge of the ruffled trim, but don't get any mix on the ruffle itself. Work quickly so that the mixture does not dry. When the wreath is covered, lift it off the bowl.

Lay the wreath on newspaper. Make a bow and wrap a chenille stem around the center of it. Poke the ends into the wreath. Push cloves into the holes inside the wreath. Wash the spoons and bowls immediately.

BEAN WREATH ORNAMENTS

The large wreath, *opposite*, is perfect for the window, wall, or front door— and it's in season all year long.

The smaller wreath, *below*, is put together just like the bigger one. Little wreaths are wonderful to tie onto packages or to decorate your Christmas tree. Leave off the ribbon hanger, and they make terrific napkin rings for your family's fall dinner table. Put some around candles for a centerpiece. You'll think of lots of ways to use them.

CINNAMON ORNAMENTS

Cinnamon cutouts are fun to make, and they add a holiday scent to any room where they are used. Make plenty to hang on the Christmas tree, on door wreaths, and in kitchen windows. Or create cinnamon decorations for any occasion—all you need to do is change cookie cutters.

GETTING STARTED

- ☐ 1 cup of ground cinnamon
- ☐ 4 tablespoons of white glue
- ☐ ¾ to 1 cup of water
- ☐ Rolling pin
- ☐ Cookie cutters
- ☐ Cookie sheet
- ☐ Toothpick
- ☐ Waxed paper
- ☐ Acrylic paint
- ☐ Artist's brush

1 DOING THE PROJECT

Stir together 1 cup of cinnamon, 4 tablespoons of white glue, and ¾ cup of water. The dough should be as thick as cookie dough.

2 Keep the dough in the refrigerator for 2 hours. Then, sprinkle cinnamon on your work surface. Spoon the chilled dough from the bowl onto the cinnamon. Use your fingers and hands to knead the dough until it is smooth. Ask an adult to show you how to knead dough if you have not done it before.

3 Sprinkle more cinnamon on the work surface. Roll the dough to about a ¼-inch thickness. Cut out the shapes with cookie cutters.

4 To dry the shapes, lay them on waxed paper at room temperature and turn them over twice a day for four days. To speed up the drying, bake the ornaments on a cookie sheet in a warm oven for 2 hours.

5 Before you dry the cinnamon ornaments, poke a hole in each one with a plastic straw. The circle of dough will pull out with the straw. When the shapes are dry, thread a ribbon hanger through each hole.

CINNAMON MOBILE

Another great project you can make from cinnamon shapes is this quick-as-a-wink mobile.

Wrap a wire or plastic clothes hanger with yarn or ribbon. Tie it with a bow at the top. Thread narrow ribbons in matching or contrasting colors through the holes in the tops of the ornaments. Hang five of the different shapes along the bottom of the hanger.

Leave the cinnamon cutouts unpainted, or decorate them like the ones on the following page.

6 FINISHING THE PROJECT

See our full-size patterns on *pages 20–21,* or make up your own designs. Use acrylic paints and an artist's brush to decorate the shapes. Let each color dry before you add the next color to the cutout.

7 The ornaments will shrink. Don't be surprised to see that the ornaments get smaller during both the oven- and natural-drying process. Keep this in mind when you pick out the cookie cutters for your designs. You will also notice that if you do not turn the ornaments over often enough while they are drying, the edges of the ornaments will curl.

CINNAMON ORNAMENTS

DESIGNS YOU KNEAD FOR
SPECIAL OCCASIONS

It's fun to make decorations for
holidays throughout the year. This chapter
has some project ideas that you can
create from dough for Easter, Halloween, and
Christmas. The dough is made from flour,
salt, and water, and although it looks like
something you might make to eat, it's
really just a kind of clay. And, making and
coloring the clay is almost as much
fun as shaping it!

DOUGH BASICS

Celebrate the changing seasons with the colorful dough decorations found on the next 14 pages.

GETTING STARTED

☐ **Basic recipe:**
  2 cups flour
  1 cup salt
  1 cup cold water

☐ **White acrylic paint**

☐ **Rolling pin**

☐ **Cookie cutters**

☐ **Paste food coloring**

☐ **Paraffin**

☐ **Garlic press**

☐ **Small black beads**

☐ **Crafts glue**

☐ **Fishing line**

☐ **Custard cups**

☐ **Paper clips; wire cutters**

1 Stir together flour, salt, and water. Knead the mixture until it forms a medium-stiff, smooth dough. If necessary, add more flour or water to reach the right consistency.

2 To add color, take a small portion of the dough and work in little dabs of paste food coloring until you reach the desired shade. For white dough, mix in white acrylic paint. Store any unused dough in plastic bags in the refrigerator until you are ready to begin working on your projects.

3 Place a small amount of flour on a waxed-paper-covered surface. Use a rolling pin to roll out the dough to ½-inch thickness. Dip the cookie cutter in flour and cut out the rabbit shapes. If you cannot find a similar cookie cutter, make a master pattern from cardboard (trace the rabbit *below*) and cut around the shape with a kitchen knife.

4 Roll some of the dough into 1-inch-diameter balls (about the size of a quarter) for the upper part of the rabbit's leg. Roll other small pieces of the dough into rope shapes as shown in the photograph, *above*. These pieces will be used for the foot extension (see *page 26* for explanation).

■ **Using acrylic white paint.** The bunny decorations here and on the following two pages use acrylic white paint to color the dough. If you have a smaller brother or sister, or if any small children will be present while you are working, skip the acrylic paint. Small children are unusually curious and often put things in their mouths. Acrylic paint could be very harmful if swallowed.

DOUGH BUNNIES

5 TO MAKE STANDING BUNNIES

Dab a little water on the smaller pieces to make them stick to the larger cutout shape.

1 2 3

■ **For the first step:** Press one ball of dough (about the size of a dime) in place for the tail. Press a larger ball in place for the hind leg. Take a 1-inch piece of the dough and roll it between your palms into a rope shape; apply it to the hind leg to form the back foot. Dip your fingers into water and smooth the leg and foot together.

■ **For the second step:** Add red food coloring to the dough to make light pink. Make a tiny ball for the nose. Roll small rope shapes for the inner ear. Flatten and press them in place. Use a blunt-end kitchen knife to make marks in the paws and tail. Press in place a small black bead for the eye and two 3-inch pieces of clear fishing line for the whiskers.

■ **For the third step:** Color a portion of the dough green. Push the green dough through the garlic press. Apply to the lower edge of the bunny.

■ **TO MAKE ORNAMENTS**
Lay the cutouts on a foil-covered cookie sheet. **Ask an adult** to cut a paper clip in half using wire cutters. Insert the cut end into the head. Or, make a hole with the end of a plastic straw for ribbon.

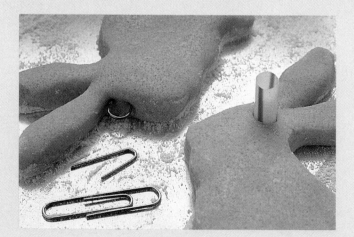

6 FINISHING THE PROJECT

Ask an adult to help you dry the bunnies in a 325° oven for one to two hours, or until the ornaments feel hard to the touch. When the bunnies have finished baking, remove the pan from the oven and place it on a wire rack to cool.

■ Hot paraffin is used next. **You must have adult help** to finish the bunnies.

■ When the wax on the bunnies has cooled, use white crafts glue to attach jelly-bean "wheels" to the front and back of each side. This will allow the bunny to stand by itself. Or, make it the center of attention in an Easter basket centerpiece, surrounded by jelly beans and candy eggs.

7

Melt the paraffin in a bowl placed in a pan of boiling water. Using a slotted spatula or spoon, dip each bunny into the melted paraffin. Transfer the bunny to a wire rack that is sitting on newspapers.

EGGS AND BASKETS

Green grass, baby chicks, and soft pastel colors are a sure sign of spring. The handmade decorations, *below*, will chase away all of your winter blahs.

GETTING STARTED

- [ ] Basic recipe:
     2 cups flour
     1 cup salt
     1 cup cold water

- [ ] Paste food coloring

- [ ] Rolling pin

- [ ] White acrylic paint

- [ ] Paraffin

- [ ] Cookie cutters

- [ ] Garlic press

- [ ] Small black beads

- [ ] Glue

- [ ] Custard cups

EASTER BASKETS

1 DOING THE PROJECT

Color a large amount of the dough bright green. Pinch off a portion and put it in the basket of the garlic press. Squeeze the dough through the press and watch the "grass grow."

■ MAKING THE EGGS

Roll each of four colors of dough into a rope; twist all four together. Flatten to ½ inch thick. Cut into egg shapes. Insert half of a paper clip into each egg; dry in a 325° oven for one hour.

2 Lay the strands along the bottom and sides of a custard cup, pressing lightly in place with your fingers. Place the filled custard cups on a cookie sheet. **Ask an adult** to help you dry them in a 325° oven for one hour. Remove the cups from the oven and cool them on a wire rack.

3 Use cookie cutters to make baby chicks or bunny face decorations for the baskets, or form them with your hands by looking at the photograph, *left*. Place the bunnies and chicks on a foil-covered cookie sheet. Press beads in place for eyes. Dry them in a 325° oven for one hour. Remove them from the oven and allow them to cool thoroughly. Use a strong, fast-drying crafts glue to adhere the chicks and bunnies to the sides of the dough baskets.

4 **FINISHING THE PROJECT**
Ask an adult to help you melt paraffin in a bowl placed in a pan of boiling water. Using a slotted spatula or spoon, dip the baskets and the eggs (one at a time) into the paraffin. Allow them to cool on a wire rack. Remember to always protect your work surface with newspapers.

HALLOWEEN PROJECTS

Roly-poly pumpkins, black cats, and witches, *below*, are quite a trio for spook's-night party favors or table decorations. Begin with the basic dough recipe on *page 24*. Step-by-step instructions for the wicked witches follow on *pages 32–33*.

GETTING STARTED

- ☐ **Basic recipe:** See *page 24*.
- ☐ **Paste food coloring**
- ☐ **Paraffin**
- ☐ **Garlic press**
- ☐ **Paper clips**
- ☐ **Small black and white beads**
- ☐ **Small magnets**
- ☐ **Clear fishing line**

JACK-O'-LANTERNS

1 DOING THE PROJECT

Make a firm ball of aluminum foil about the size of a golf ball. Color a large amount of the dough bright orange. (One cup of dough should make one pumpkin.) Use a rolling pin to roll some of the dough into a circle. The circle should measure three times as large as the foil ball and about ½ inch thick. Place the foil ball in the center and lift the dough, wrapping and pressing to cover the foil.

2

Trim any excess dough from the top so that it now looks like the ball in Step 2, *above*. Press the surface smooth with your fingertips. With a toothpick, poke holes in the bottom of the pumpkin so that the paraffin can drain when the pumpkin is dipped in wax.

3

Make cardboard patterns for the eyes, nose, and mouth. (See Step 3, *above*.) Press the shapes into the dough to make impressions, then remove the cardboard. Use a toothpick to mark vertical lines in the jack-o'-lantern's sides. Use a small amount of green dough to make a stem; press it into place. Dry the pumpkins on a foil-covered cookie sheet in a 325° oven for one to two hours, or until hard. Dip cooled pumpkins in paraffin, following the directions on *page 27*.

BLACK CAT

1 DOING THE PROJECT

To make a cat magnet, tint dough in black, orange, and green. Cut out black cat shape. Add fishing-line whiskers. Use two small balls of orange-tinted dough to form small pumpkins; decorate with black eyes, nose, and mouth. Dry in a 325° oven until firm; dip in paraffin to seal. Glue a magnet to the back.

DOUGH WITCH HEADS

1 DOING THE PROJECT
Shape a small handful of light brown-tinted dough into a 2-inch oval ball for the face. Attach a flattened piece for the neck.

2 Use untinted dough for the eyebrows and hair. Push the dough through the garlic press to form strands. Attach the hair to the head. (Our drawings are full-size.)

3 Poke two small black beads into the head for the eyes. **Ask an adult** to help you carve out a mouth shape. Push several tiny white beads into the mouth for teeth, positioning them at random. Shape a very pointed nose and attach it to the face. Top it off with a small dough wart.

4 Make tiny balls of light brown-tinted dough for warts. Place them on the chin and cheeks, and around the eyes. Press two flattened circles of pink dough on the cheeks. Be as creative as you want to be when you make the faces. Make some witches happy and some very scary.

5 FINISHING THE PROJECT
Roll black dough into an 8-inch circle about ¼ inch thick; cut the circle in half. Shape a half-circle into a cone around the witch's head, pinching the ends together at the head back. Pull the bottom in place so that it flares out over the hair. Add a hatband made from orange dough. Insert one-half of a paper clip for hanging. Dry in a 325° oven for one or two hours, or until hard. Dip in hot paraffin following the directions on *page 27*.

CHRISTMAS PROJECTS

'Tis the season to be merry, and what could make a friend happier than these wonderful Christmas decorations made in your own kitchen. Ask Mom to let you look at her cookie cutters for Christmas designs, or use the suggestions on these pages. Hang the stockings from the fireplace. Trim packages with smaller dough cutouts, and decorate potted Christmas cactus and poinsettias with ornaments on bamboo skewers.

GETTING STARTED

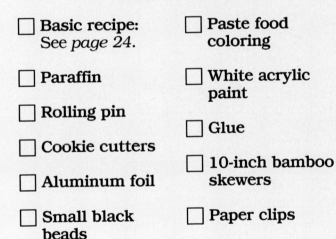

☐ **Basic recipe:** See *page 24.*

☐ **Paraffin**

☐ **Rolling pin**

☐ **Cookie cutters**

☐ **Aluminum foil**

☐ **Small black beads**

☐ **Paste food coloring**

☐ **White acrylic paint**

☐ **Glue**

☐ **10-inch bamboo skewers**

☐ **Paper clips**

A FAMILY OF CHRISTMAS BEARS

1 DOING THE PROJECT
Mix together one batch of the basic bread dough recipe given in Step 1, *page 24.* Color some of the dough red and some green. Mix a second batch of the dough, adding white acrylic paint for color.

2 Use a rolling pin to roll out the white dough to about ½ inch thickness. Cut out various sizes of teddy bears. Use bits of red and green tinted dough to make bow ties, hearts, holly leaves, and berries to decorate the bears. Push small black beads into the dough to form the bears' eyes.

3 To make bear shapes stick in potted plants, insert a 10-inch bamboo skewer into the cutouts before they are dried.

4 FINISHING THE PROJECT
Bake in a 325° oven for one to two hours, or until hard. Coat with paraffin, following the instructions on *page 27.*

CANDY CANES

1 DOING THE PROJECT
Color one portion of homemade dough with white acrylic paint. Tint another portion with red coloring. Roll equal-size pieces of each color into ropes and twist them together.

2 FINISHING THE PROJECT
Cut the twisted strip to the desired lengths; bend one end to make the curved top. Dry candy canes in a 325° oven for one to two hours. Dip in paraffin to coat.

CHRISTMAS STOCKINGS

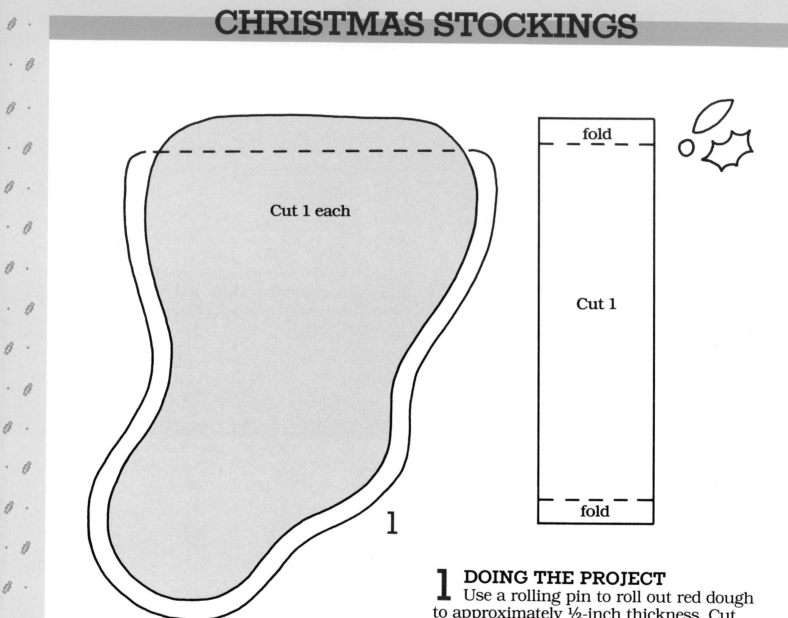

Cut 1 each

fold

Cut 1

1

fold

1

■ **Cutting out the pattern.** The stocking pattern, *above,* actually represents two pieces. The shaded portion is the stocking back. The outside solid line is the cutting line for the front piece.

1 DOING THE PROJECT
Use a rolling pin to roll out red dough to approximately ½-inch thickness. Cut a stocking front and a stocking back from cardboard. Lay the cardboard shapes on the red dough and cut out both pieces. Roll out white-tinted dough. Use the pattern, *above,* to cut out the stocking cuff. Press it in place on the stocking top. Shape and attach green dough holly leaves and red dough berries to the cuff.

2 Crumple a piece of aluminum foil small enough to fit inside the toe and foot of the stocking. Lay the foil on the bottom piece of dough. Place the stocking top on the foil and mold the top down over the foil around the toe and heel area. Crumple a second piece of foil to hold the stocking top open. Place it between the top and bottom. Pinch together the sides, leaving the top open. Smooth the edges where the top and back are joined.

3 FINISHING THE PROJECT
Insert one-half of a paper clip into both upper corners of the back piece. If you choose, use an artist's paintbrush and acrylic paint or a permanent marker to write a name on the cuff. Lay the stocking on a foil-covered baking sheet. Bake in a 375° oven one to two hours, or until hard. Remove the top foil. Ask an adult to help you coat the stocking with paraffin, following the directions on *page 27*.

VALENTINES THAT SAY "BE MINE"

Valentine's Day is a time for us to show affection to friends and those we love. It's fun to give valentine greetings every February, and even more fun when you can give a valentine that you've made yourself.
The collection of ideas in this chapter begins with some easy hearts—just some pretty papers, glue, and a little imagination are all you need to start. There are also fancy valentines for you to make for those extra-special people on your list.

VALENTINES

Making and giving cards that you've made yourself make Valentine's Day more fun. Start with paper doilies or paper hearts, and add your favorite stickers or cutouts from old greeting cards. Trim the valentines with glitter or ribbons.

GETTING STARTED

- [ ] Construction paper
- [ ] Stickers
- [ ] Greeting cards
- [ ] Paper doilies
- [ ] Ribbons
- [ ] Glitter
- [ ] Crafts glue
- [ ] Scissors
- [ ] Silver and gold foil

CANDY HEARTS

Here's a fun way to give a candy-filled valentine. Use different shapes for other occasions—such as a star for a friend's birthday.

GETTING STARTED

☐ Construction paper

☐ Clear adhesive-backed vinyl

☐ Heavy clear plastic

☐ Scissors, yarn

☐ Single-hole paper punch

☐ Assorted candies

1 DOING THE PROJECT

Make a heart-shape paper pattern from a 6-inch square of paper. Cut it out. Trace around this shape onto construction paper.

Cut a 6-inch square of clear adhesive-backed vinyl. Remove the backing paper and stick it onto the construction paper. Cut out the heart shape. Cut out a heart from the clear plastic.

2 Put both the clear vinyl heart and the paper heart together with the clear heart on top. Using a single-hole paper punch, make holes around the edges of the heart pieces. Try to keep the holes evenly spaced and the same distance from the edges. Hold the hearts tightly together to keep them from sliding.

■ *Applying clear adhesive-backed vinyl.*
With practice, you can put the adhesive-backed vinyl on the construction paper so that there are no bubbles or wrinkles. Pull off the corner of the paper backing. Line up the sticky corner with the corner of the construction paper. Pull off the rest of the backing and press down.

3 To assemble the heart pieces, place the vinyl heart on top of the covered paper heart, making sure the holes line up. Cut a 36-inch piece of yarn. Begin "sewing" the pieces together by pulling the yarn through the hole at the top of the heart. Leave about 8 inches loose to tie the bow. (To keep it out of your way while you work, tape it to the back side.) Pull it through the next hole to make a stitch. Continue around the edge until you've gone past the bottom point of the heart.

4 FINISHING THE PROJECT

Fill the heart with candy. Then, continue stitching the pieces together until you reach the top. With the end of yarn you left free at the beginning, tie a bow to keep the heart closed. Too much candy will make the heart curl up and look lumpy. Undo a few stitches and take out some candy if this happens.

CROSS-STITCH PINCUSHION

Cross-stitch embroidery is very easy. Fabric that already has squares marked for stitching can be purchased at stores that carry needlework supplies. An "X" is made by going up and down through holes on the four corners of each square. Make sure the first stitch in each "X" always goes in the same direction. The stitch diagram, *opposite, bottom*, will show you how.

GETTING STARTED

☐ **Embroidery floss**

☐ **8x8-inch fabric for backing**

☐ **Scissors, tapestry needle**

☐ **8-inch square of 11-count Aida cloth**

☐ **Stuffing:** We used polyester fiberfill.

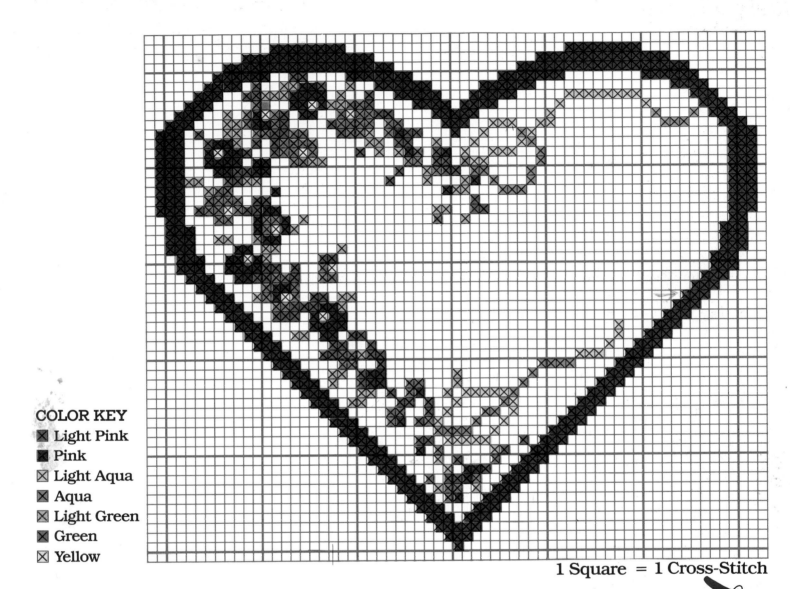

COLOR KEY
☒ Light Pink
■ Pink
☒ Light Aqua
☒ Aqua
☒ Light Green
☒ Green
☒ Yellow

1 Square = 1 Cross-Stitch

1 DOING THE PROJECT

Use the pattern, *above,* for the pincushion design. Pick embroidery floss colors to match the color key. Make one stitch for every square.

2 FINISHING THE PROJECT

To make the pincushion shown on the opposite page, pin the embroidered front to a backing with right sides facing.

3

Sew just outside the stitches. Leave a 2-inch opening. Trim the edges, turn it right side out, and stuff. Sew the opening closed.

CROSS-STITCH

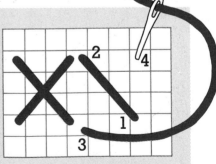

■ **Making the stitch.** Follow the diagram, *right.* Come up through the fabric at 1 and go back down at 2.

■ **Finishing the stitch.** Come up at 3 and back down at 4. Repeat for all stitches.

BUNNY CARDS

A simple cutout shape like this bunny makes a very pretty valentine for your family and friends. As the card is opened, two bunnies and a heart appear! The area inside the card gives enough space for adding your own greeting.

GETTING STARTED

☐ **Scissors**

☐ **Paper:** Medium-weight watercolor paper, cut to 12x7 inches.

☐ **Crayons**

☐ **Tracing paper**

☐ **Paper punch**

☐ **Pencil**

☐ **Cotton balls**

☐ **Crafts glue**

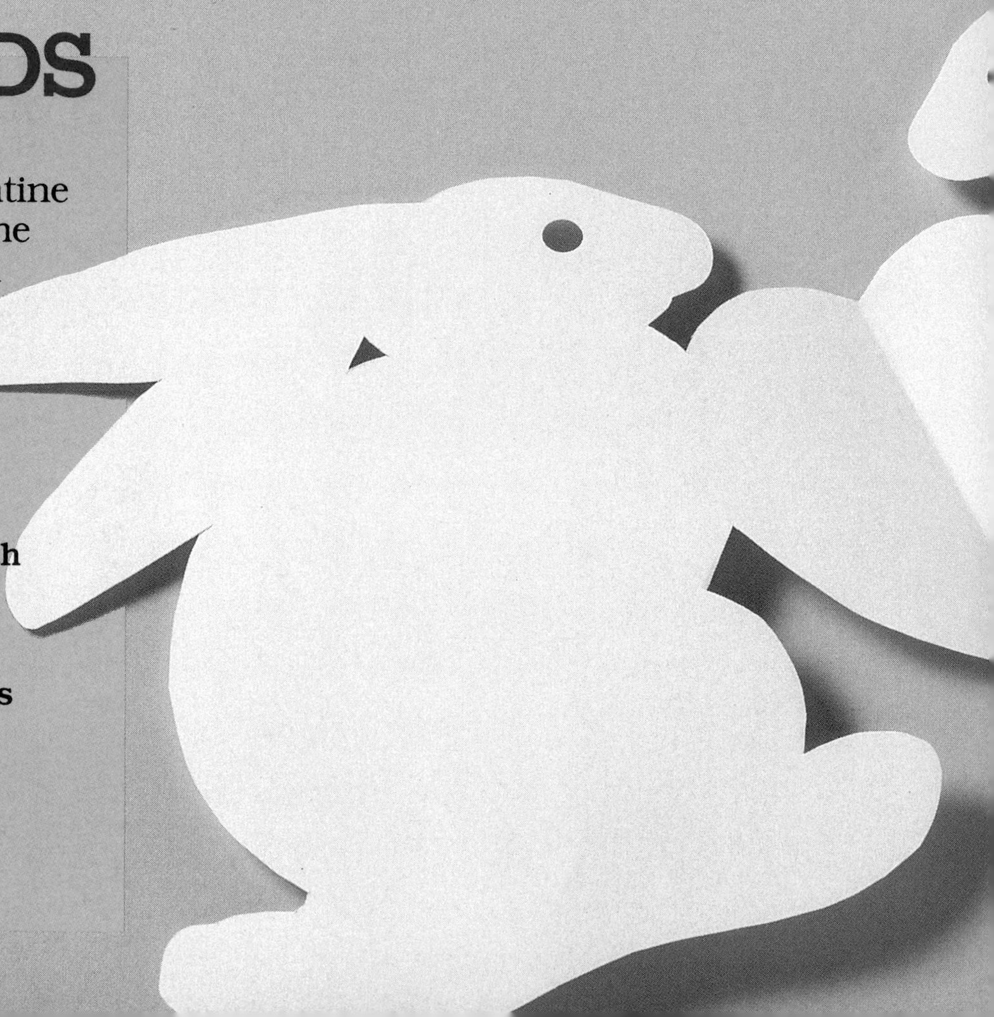

4

3

1 DOING THE PROJECT

With tracing paper, copy the bunny pattern on *page 50*. Fold the watercolor paper in half to form a 6x7-inch rectangle. Cut out the bunny pattern and place it on the folded paper, lining up the middle of the heart on the paper's fold. Trace around the bunny shape and draw in the dotted lines.

2

Keeping the paper folded, cut out the card along the outline. Using a paper punch, make eyes. Color the heart and inside of the bunny's ears with crayons; make a nose.

3

Open up the card and write the valentine greeting on one of the bunny shapes. Sign your name at the bottom. Add the date, if there's room.

4

Finish coloring the front of the card by adding a mouth, whiskers, lines between the toes, and lines between the ears and legs. Put a small drop of glue on the tail and stick on a single cotton ball. Let the glue dry.

Happy Valentine's Day Mom From: Ann

CUT-PAPER HEART

It's easy to make a heart shape by folding a sheet of paper in half and cutting it out. The valentine, *opposite*, is made exactly the same way but has additional cutout flowers around the edges.

GETTING STARTED

- [ ] **Paper:** Use lightweight watercolor paper.
- [ ] **Transfer paper**
- [ ] **Pencil**
- [ ] **Glue stick**
- [ ] **Colored pens**
- [ ] **Scissors**
- [ ] **Mat-board backing**
- [ ] **Frame**

2 Unfold the paper and put the inside surface up. Color the heart and flowers with colored pens. Put a piece of scrap paper under your work so that you can color right up to the edges of the shapes. Make a smaller heart with a valentine greeting to fit inside the scalloped heart.

1 DOING THE PROJECT

Fold an 8x10-inch piece of paper in half to measure 5x8 inches. Trace the pattern on *page 51* onto one side. Cut out through both layers.

3 FINISHING THE PROJECT

Cut a piece of mat-board backing to fit inside a frame. Turn the cut-paper heart over and apply glue to the back with a glue stick. Again, be sure to work on scrap paper. Center the valentine on the mat board and press it down firmly.

VALENTINE PROJECTS

■ **Bunny card pattern.** Use the pattern, *below,* for the Bunny Cards pictured on *pages 46–47.* Notice the dotted line along the middle of the heart. When this is lined up correctly with the fold of the paper, a heart is formed as the card is opened and another bunny appears.

■ **Cut-paper valentine pattern.** Use the pattern, *opposite,* for the framed valentine on *pages 48–49.* You'll only need to trace half of this pattern to make the entire design.

fold

– – – **Drawing lines**
—— **Cutting lines**

TOP

fold

fold

– – – Drawing lines
——— Cutting lines

PATTERN PORTFOLIO

On the next 14 pages, we've given you
oodles of our own funny doodles from A to Z.
Use the alphabet and the drawings
to make lots of crafts projects for just about
any occasion. Then see how many
more things you can think of that begin with
each letter.

A IS FOR: **A**RK

B IS FOR:

BIRD

BUTTERFLY

BAT

BEARS

C IS FOR:

Camel

Cows

Cats

D IS FOR:

DUCKS

DONKEY

DOGS

E IS FOR: ELEPHANTS

F IS FOR: FISH

G IS FOR:

GHOST

GIRAFFE

GOOSE

H IS FOR:

HOUSE

HIPPOPOTAMUS

HORSE

I IS FOR:

ICE-CREAM CONES

J IS FOR:

JACKRABBITS

K IS FOR:

KITE

L IS FOR:

LADYBUG

LIONS

M IS FOR:

MONKEY

MOOSE

MOUSE

N IS FOR:

NEST

O IS FOR:

OWLS

P IS FOR:

PIGS

Q IS FOR:

R IS FOR:

Rooster

Queen

Reindeer

S IS FOR:

SHEEP

SQUIRREL

T IS FOR:

TIGER

TURKEY

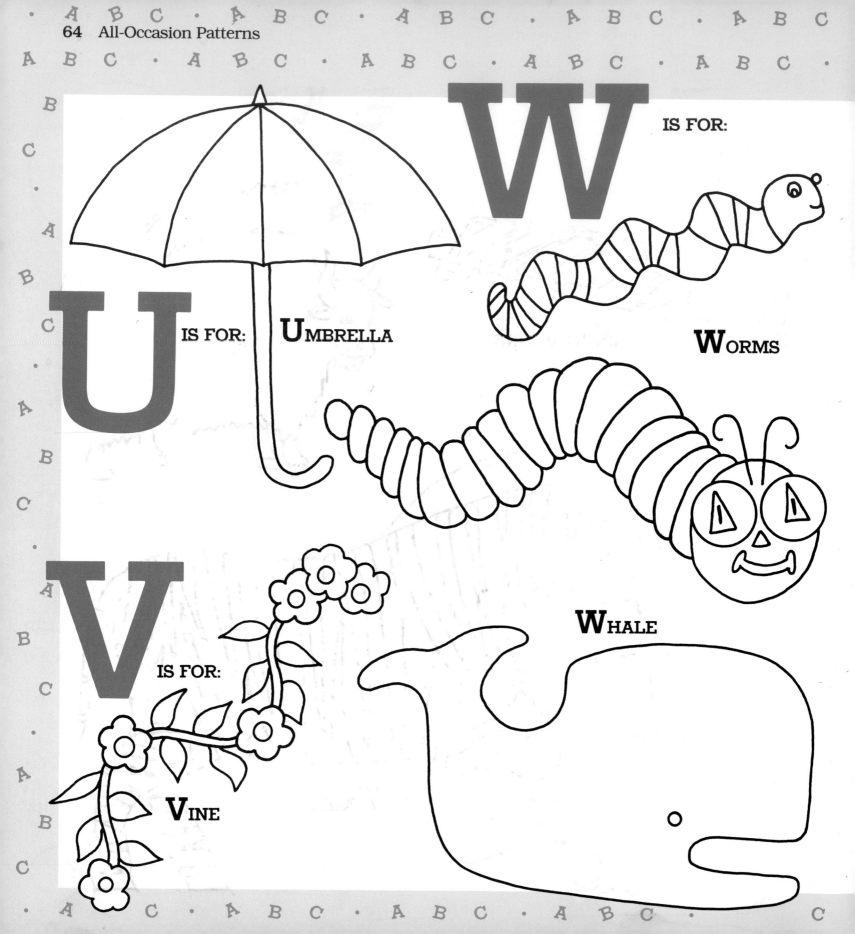

U IS FOR: **U**MBRELLA

W IS FOR:

WORMS

V IS FOR:

VINE

WHALE

X IS FOR:

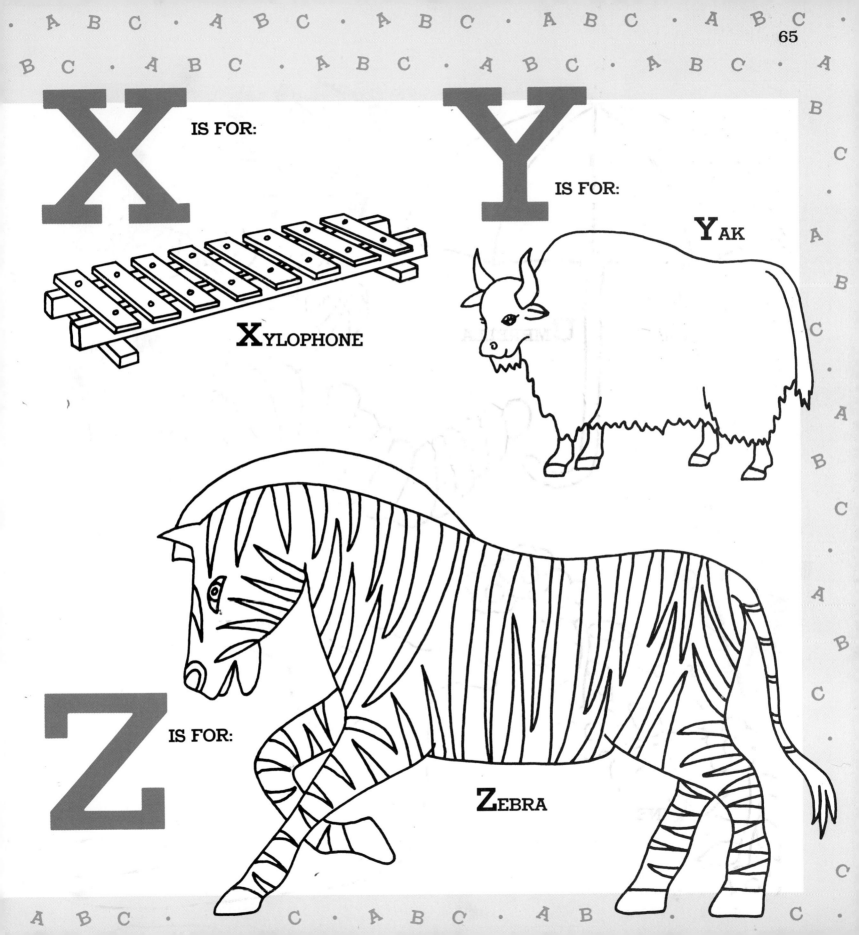

XYLOPHONE

Y IS FOR:

YAK

Z IS FOR:

ZEBRA

MAY DAY SURPRISES

May Day festivities
have been around for a long time—it's
always been a day to celebrate the coming
of spring and new growth. It's a
time to make new friends, too, and one
way we do that is by exchanging
May baskets.
This chapter has special things
to make and share with your old and
new friends on this holiday. It includes
easy baskets to craft from pretty papers and
ways to trim them with stickers.

SURPRISING ROLL-UPS

Cardboard tubes covered with crepe paper and decorated with colorful stickers are loaded with wonderfully sweet confections for May Day giving. Turn the page for other ideas that will make May a month to remember.

GETTING STARTED

☐ **Cardboard tubes** ☐ **Crinkle ribbon**

☐ **Scissors** ☐ **Stickers**

☐ **Crepe paper**

2 Cut one 20-inch length of crepe paper for each May basket. The longer edges of the 10x20-inch piece of paper can be stretched easily. Using your forefingers and your thumbs, carefully pull (or stretch) the crepe paper at 1-inch intervals to form a ruffled edge.

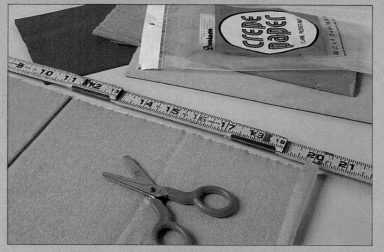

1 DOING THE PROJECT

Cut cardboard tubes saved from gift wrap, paper towels, waxed paper, or bathroom tissue into 3½-inch lengths. Cut crepe paper into two 10-inch sections.

4 FINISHING THE PROJECT

Fill the tube with popcorn and candy treats. Tie the second end of the ribbon length to the other end of the paper-covered tube. This will form a handle for the May basket and will hold the treats inside. Pull the ruffled ends of the crepe paper apart to form a "flower." Curl streamers of paper ribbon using the edge of your scissors and tie them to the ends. Last, but certainly not least, add one of your favorite stickers.

3

Wrap the paper around the cardboard tube. Pinch the paper together at one end and tic it securely using one end of a 20-inch length of ribbon.

MAY BASKETS AND CONES

Here are two more May Day designs that are fun to make and give to friends. Use the same materials for both styles. Only the pattern is different.

GETTING STARTED

- ☐ **Medium-weight paper:** We used Color Cast from an art supplies store.
- ☐ **Tracing paper**
- ☐ **Pencil**
- ☐ **Ruler**
- ☐ **Scissors**
- ☐ **Crafts glue**
- ☐ **Stickers**

DOING THE PROJECT

1 Trace the full-size pattern on *page 75* onto tissue paper. Using carbon paper and a pencil, transfer the pattern to the back side of the colored paper.

2 Cut out the entire basket shape and cut inward along the bottom on all solid lines as marked on the pattern. Fold the basket along **all** dotted lines.

FINISHING THE PROJECT
Refold and glue the basket along the side flap. Fold the bottom together and glue the bottom flap in place. Cut a ½x6-inch strip of paper for the handle. Glue the strip in place on two sides of the basket. Add the stickers.

STICKERS

You can decorate almost anything with stickers. There are pretty ones, cute ones, and just plain silly ones.

We have used stickers here and throughout this book to make gifts more personal. If you know someone who especially likes cats, geese, or teddy bears, pick out a sticker with one of those animals on it and put it on your handmade gift.

There are stickers that glitter or glow in the dark. You can even buy scratch-and-sniff stickers that smell like your favorite treats. Part of the fun is looking at the variety.

MAY DAY CONES

The cone shapes, shown *below* and *opposite,* use the same materials that were used in the baskets on *pages 70–71.* (See the materials list on *page 70.*) The only difference is the shape. Use the pattern on *page 74* and follow the simple instructions, *below.*

1 DOING THE PROJECT
Trace the pattern on *page 74* onto tissue paper. Transfer the pattern to the back side of medium-weight paper. Mark the dotted pattern lines on the back of your colored paper. Cut along the solid outline only.

2 FINISHING THE PROJECT
Put a thin layer of glue along one side. Let the glue set long enough to become tacky, then press the two sides together. Cut a ½x6-inch paper handle and glue it in place.

MAY DAY SURPRISES

Once the baskets are made, fill them with sweet surprises. On the first day of May, put them on someone's front step, ring the doorbell, and watch faces light up with delight.

MAY BASKETS AND CONES

■ **Cutting out the shapes.** Cut out the pieces along the solid lines only. On the bottom of the box shape, *opposite,* this will include cutting upward to the sides. The dotted line on the box pattern represents the fold lines. The dotted line on the cone pattern, *below,* shows you where to put the glue and where to overlap the two sides.

Place glue here

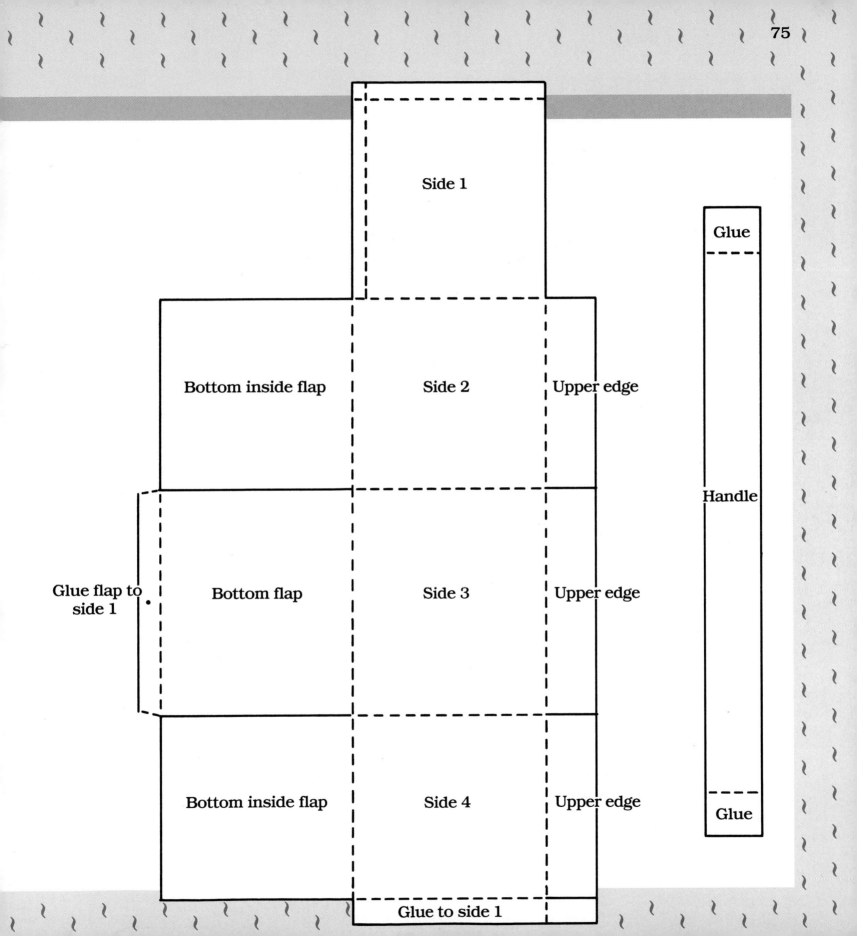

Side 1

Bottom inside flap | Side 2 | Upper edge

Glue flap to side 1 | Bottom flap | Side 3 | Upper edge

Bottom inside flap | Side 4 | Upper edge

Glue to side 1

Glue

Handle

Glue

A SPECIAL GIFT TO
WELCOME BABY

The arrival of a baby sister or brother
is a big event for your family. If you'd like
to make a present for Mom, Dad,
and the new baby, this chapter has a few
ideas for you. The projects are made
from plain paper that's decorated in a special
way. First, you'll cut out shapes (such as
birds and flowers) from white paper,
and then add designs by making small holes
in the paper with needles. You might have
to ask an adult to help you with some
of the steps, but you'll have a present that
Mom and Dad will be proud of.

PIERCED PAPER GIFTS

You can make a special gift for your newest family member with paper, scissors, and a sewing needle.

GETTING STARTED

- ☐ Purchased 8- or 9-inch grapevine wreath
- ☐ Lightweight, watercolor paper
- ☐ Tissue paper
- ☐ Pencil
- ☐ Masking tape
- ☐ Foam pad
- ☐ Sewing needles in assorted sizes
- ☐ White crafts glue
- ☐ Flat white spray paint
- ☐ 1½ yards of narrow ribbon in two colors

1 DOING THE PROJECT

Buy an 8- or 9-inch grapevine wreath and paint it with a flat white spray paint.

2 Trace the patterns on *pages 82–83* onto tissue paper. Tape the patterns onto the watercolor paper. Use a foam pad and poke holes with a needle following the marks on the pattern.

3 Leave the tissue pattern taped to the watercolor paper and cut around the outside edges of all of the pieces. Glue the wings in place to the bird bodies.

4 **FINISHING THE PROJECT**
With all of the wings glued to the bird bodies and all of the heart shapes cut out, simply glue them in place to finish your gift.

■ **Adding the ribbons.** Use the photograph, *opposite*, to guide you in adding colorful pastel ribbons to the wreath. Weave the narrow ribbon in and around the vines, paper birds, and hearts. Adding both pink and blue ribbons lets you make the present even before the baby arrives.

PICTURE FRAMES

1 **DOING THE PROJECT**
The colorful mat, *above*, is the perfect way to frame the first picture of the new baby. It is even more special because you made it yourself.

■ Most crafts and frame shops carry picture mattings that are already cut and come in a good variety of colors and sizes. Pick one you like with either a rectangle or an oval shape cut out of the center. If the baby's picture will be taken by a photographer, ask Mom and Dad which size frame will be best for the picture they will buy.

2 Make the hearts and birds just like you did for the paper wreath, *opposite*. You may use any of the shapes. Pick out the smallest hearts and birds if you are working on a small mat.

3 **FINISHING THE PROJECT**
Glue the hearts and bird in place on the mat. Make a ribbon bow with streamers to glue to the birds' beaks. Glue the ends of the ribbon to two of the hearts. It will look like the bird is flying around spreading hearts of love over the picture.

NOTE CARDS

1 **DOING THE PROJECT**
You can make cards, birth announcements, gift tags, bookmarks, and more using the patterns for the birds and hearts.

■ Cut and fold watercolor paper or stationery to the size you want for your card or tag. Decide where you want the design to be.

2 Remember that the design shows up best when you poke the holes from the back side of the paper. If you want the shape to appear on the right corner of the finished card, you will punch the left corner of the back side.

3 **FINISHING THE PROJECT**
Use a paper punch to make a hole in the bookmark top. Loop ribbon through the hole. Mom can use the bookmark to keep her place when writing information in the baby book.

PAPER BIRDS AND HEARTS

Making birds and hearts. Always tape your pattern, facedown, onto the back side of the watercolor paper. You will then be poking holes from back to front. When you turn the paper over to the right side, the punched holes stand out clearly.

PLEASE DON'T EAT THE
VEGETABLES

Because vegetables grow in a variety of sizes, shapes, and textures, they are perfect for printmaking. In this chapter, we show you how to cut a vegetable in just the right way, how to coat the surface with paint, and then how to press it on a flat surface to get a copy, or "impression," of the shape. These shapes can be used to decorate paper and fabric. With a little help, you can turn your artwork into great gifts—and even make the wrapping paper to wrap your gifts in.

■ **Radish:** Leaving a piece of the root gives a "stem" print.

■ **Pepper:** Vertical cut leaves a hollow oval shape.

■ **Mushroom:** Hollow stems create outlines.

■ **Cauliflower:** Looks like a small tree.

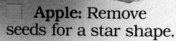
■ **Apple:** Remove seeds for a star shape.

1 DOING THE PROJECT

Ask an adult to help you cut the fruits and vegetables. Allow the halves to dry on paper towels for at least one hour. Dried fruits and vegetables should be used within two days.

■ Remember that lemons, oranges, onions, and zucchini should dry for two to five days before you use them for printing.

Lemon: Allow to dry two days.

Pepper: Horizontal cut, leaving the center, makes compartments.

Carrot: Makes neat round circles in a variety of sizes.

VEGETABLE PRINTING

Half the fun of printing with fruits and vegetables is experimenting with shapes and colors. Designs are limited only by your imagination. Here we show you a few of the patterns you can print using some familiar foods. Below are suggestions for other fruits and vegetables that make interesting prints.

GETTING STARTED

☐ Oranges	☐ Celery
☐ Acorn squash	☐ Onions
☐ Potato	☐ Zucchini

2 Cover your worktable with old newspapers. Choose a brush that is easy to hold. Dip the tip into paint, being careful not to get too much paint on the bristles. Brush paint on the cut edge of the fruit or vegetable.

PRINTING ON PAPER

Vegetable printing is a plan-ahead project. Ask an adult to be on hand to help you with the cutting of the fruits and vegetables.

You may print on either paper or fabric. Paper is especially easy to work with, because you will have no rough edges to hem.

GETTING STARTED

☐ **Vegetables and fruits**

☐ **Kitchen knife:** Ask for adult help with cutting.

☐ **Watercolor paper**

☐ **Clear adhesive-backed vinyl**

☐ **Fabric paint**

☐ **Small brushes**

☐ **Small roller**

☐ **Newspaper**

☐ **Paper towels**

■ TO MAKE A PLACE MAT

For this project you will need one 12x18-inch sheet of medium-weight watercolor paper from an art store and one 12x18-inch sheet of clear adhesive-backed vinyl (like clear Con-Tact) for each place mat. To make the repeat design shown, use different sizes of one fruit or vegetable. We chose a mushroom. Cut one half for each color of paint that you want to use. Mushrooms look totally different if you cut them from top to bottom or side to side. Be sure to use some of each shape. Keep your brushes in a cup of water between paintings.

1 DOING THE PROJECT

Brush the cut surface of the mushroom with paint. Be careful not to get too much paint on the brush. Take your time when laying the mushroom down on the paper so that the design does not smudge. You can get two or three prints before you need to repaint.

2

Let the paint dry. Peel away the backing on the plastic, removing only a small portion at a time, and place the sticky side down on the paper. Use a roller to keep air bumps from forming under the plastic.

VEGETABLE PRINTING ON MUSLIN FABRIC

Printing on fabric is just like printing on paper. A 100% cotton fabric such as muslin works best because paint tends to bleed when used on polyester blends. Spread the fabric on top of four or five layers of newspaper to absorb the excess paint. Use fresh newspaper whenever you move the fabric to keep the back side of the fabric clean. When you are finished painting and the paint is dry, lay the fabric facedown on paper towels. **Ask an adult** to help you iron the back side to heat-set the paint.

GETTING STARTED

- ☐ Fruits and vegetables
- ☐ Kitchen knife: Ask for adult help, please.
- ☐ 9x9-inch muslin squares
- ☐ 9x9-inch piece of batting
- ☐ Fabric paint
- ☐ Small brushes
- ☐ Newspapers
- ☐ Iron
- ☐ Embroidery hoop
- ☐ Embroidery needle
- ☐ Quilting thread
- ☐ Bias binding

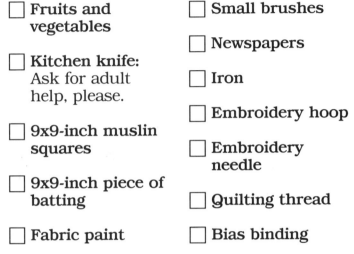

1 DOING THE PROJECT

Paint the cut edge of a dried apple half. To make the pot holder, *opposite,* print nine apples on one 9x9-inch muslin square, alternating colors. Paint one side of a seed brown and print on the apples. **Ask an adult** to help you iron the back side to heat-set the design.

2 FINISHING THE PROJECT

Sandwich the pot-holder top, batting, and backing together with the batting on the inside. Baste the edges. Place the fabrics in a quilting hoop and sew around each apple print, stitching through all three layers. **Ask an adult** to help you sew bias tape around the edges.

VEGETABLE PRINTING

There are lots of ways to print on fabric and paper—silk screening, batiking, tie-dyeing, and wood-block printing are just a few. But the simplest technique is the one we have shown you on the preceding pages. After you have learned to vegetable-print, a mushroom will never again look like just a mushroom to you. Walk through the produce department of the grocery store or take a trip to the family garden—and let your imagination work for you.

FRAMED FLORALS. The flowers in both of the framed prints, *opposite*, use acorn squash with carrot-half centers. Make the stems with carrot sticks and the leaves with radish halves. Use a wedge of cabbage for the flower bowl in the larger of the two pictures, *opposite*. Make the small five-petal flowers with broccoli stems.

LANDSCAPES AND BORDERS. To make a clever scene like the one *below*, print cauliflower trees, broccoli bushes, a carrot-section sun, cabbage hills, and a celery-stick fence. Or, decorate purchased place mats, *below*, with green peppers and lemons cut both horizontally and diagonally. Choose colors that look nice with your family's dishes.

LASTING BOUQUETS FOR MOTHER'S DAY

Drying and pressing real flowers
is a way to make their beauty last for a long,
long time. This chapter tells you how
to make a simple flower press that will
preserve certain kinds of fresh flowers and
leaves. Then you can make
note cards, bookmarks, and other gifts
with the flowers you've saved.

FLOWER PRESS

On Mother's Day, show your mother what a special person she is by giving her a gift of flowers that will stay beautiful all year long. Make a surprise bouquet for Grandma, too.

GETTING STARTED

- ☐ Two 8-inch squares of ½-inch plywood

- ☐ Four ¼-inch carriage bolts (4 inches long)

- ☐ Four ¼-inch wing nuts

- ☐ Eight ¼-inch flat washers

- ☐ Unprinted newsprint

- ☐ Twenty 8x8-inch squares of white felt

- ☐ Corrugated cardboard

- ☐ Flowers, stems, and leaves

1 DOING THE PROJECT

Ask an adult to help you build the press by following the directions, *opposite.* Layer materials in the press in this order: cardboard, felt, newsprint, flowers and leaves, and newsprint. Repeat, ending with cardboard. Use only flowers with one layer of petals. When flowers are in place, add the top piece of plywood and tighten the screws.

MAKING A FLOWER PRESS

1 Tape two 8-inch squares of plywood together.

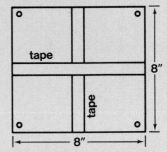

■ Measure ½ inch in from each edge and drill a ¼-inch hole through each corner. Remove the tape.

2 Cut cardboard, felt, and unprinted newsprint into 8-inch squares.

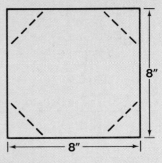

■ Trim off all corners at 45-degree angles.

3 Place a ¼-inch flat washer on a carriage bolt. Push it up through the bottom piece of plywood.

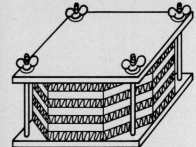

■ Fill the press.

■ Top with the second piece of plywood. Slip a washer over the end of each bolt. Tighten with a wing nut.

PRESSED FLOWER PROJECTS

Allow flowers and leaves to dry for three to six weeks. They will feel like paper when they are dry and may change color slightly in the process. Once flowers are dried and removed from the press, store them between pages of the newsprint in large envelopes. Mark each envelope with the name of the flower or leaf inside.

GETTING STARTED

- ☐ White glue
- ☐ Toothpicks
- ☐ Tweezers
- ☐ Scissors
- ☐ Adhesive-backed clear vinyl
- ☐ Colored paper and envelopes
- ☐ Paper punch
- ☐ Heavy white watercolor paper
- ☐ Iron: Ask for adult help.

1 DOING THE PROJECT

Practice arranging flowers and leaves in pleasing patterns on a scrap of paper. (See *pages 104–105* for ideas.) Choose a color of paper that will show off the flowers you are using. To make cards, fold and cut the paper to measure the same size as your envelope.

2

Squirt out a drop of glue on scratch paper. Dip one end of a toothpick in glue and place a small drop on the back of each flower. Carefully transfer the flowers and leaves to the colored paper. Center the flowers, or put them along one side to leave space to write a note.

■ ASK FOR ADULT HELP

When instructions for finishing your gift call for the use of a hot iron, please ask an adult to help with that step. Choosing the proper iron temperature is most important to the success of your project. Make certain the iron is out of the reach of smaller brothers or sisters. And don't forget to turn the iron off immediately after use.

3 As you add each glued flower back to the design, carefully press it in place using the tip of your finger. You may wish to do several note cards or bookmarks and allow them to dry thoroughly before going on to the next step.

4 When the glue is dry, cut a piece of clear adhesive-backed vinyl that measures ¼ inch larger all around than your bookmark or the front of your folded card. Peel off the protective paper. Starting at the top of the design, carefully cover the project with the vinyl. Remember: The vinyl is sticky and cannot be moved once it touches the paper or flowers.

5 FINISHING THE PROJECT
Finally, trim off the excess vinyl. Trim the cards ¼ inch smaller than the envelopes so they slip inside easily. Place projects, vinyl side up, between two sheets of heavy white paper. **Ask an adult to help** you turn the iron on to a cotton setting and press for 2 to 3 seconds.

BOUQUETS THAT LAST

Now that you have learned how much fun drying and preserving flowers can be, the possibilities are endless. Create greeting cards that open at the bottom or side just by changing the direction of the design. Or, buy a ready-made frame and pop in a card for hanging.

Make a bookmark and wrap it with a book by your mother's favorite author for a wonderful Mother's Day surprise.

■ Pansies, single hydrangea blossoms, and fern leaves

■ Cornflowers with fern leaves; daisies with geranium buds; violas, geranium buds, and Queen-Anne's-lace

■ Hydrangeas, violas, and fern leaves

■ Orange and yellow cosmos, Queen-Anne's-lace, and a butterfly

■ White daisies

■ Spiderwort with baby's breath

■ Wild rose flowers, buds, and leaves

■ Larkspur with fern leaves

GIFTS FROM NATURE'S BOUNTY

This chapter has some ideas for projects that
will teach you to use those wonderful
materials that nature has given us. You'll
learn to make ornaments from all
kinds of seeds and to decorate plain
items with leaf designs.
Start now to watch for your crafting
materials each time you walk down a country
lane or through your own backyard.
And, this may well be the last time you throw
away the seeds when you eat watermelon,
apples, and oranges!

SEED ORNAMENTS

If you've ever been to a seed and nursery store with your mom and dad, you may remember all of the flower and vegetable seeds that are sold there. The Christmas ornaments shown here and on the next two pages use those same seeds—and some common kitchen spices like dillweed and poppy seeds—as their main material for crafting.

Make a whole set for your Christmas tree, and you won't have to wait until spring to enjoy the harvest.

GETTING STARTED

☐ **Assorted seeds:** We used melon, squash, poppy, sunflower, dill, sesame, and apple seeds, plus split peas, tapioca, and hulled oats.

☐ **White crafts glue**

☐ Cardboard

☐ Gold cording

☐ Scissors

☐ Pencil

☐ Tracing paper

1 DOING THE PROJECT

Trace the bell and heart patterns from *pages 164–165* of the pattern portfolio onto tracing paper. Cut out the pattern pieces. Draw around the bell and heart on cardboard. Cut out the cardboard shapes.

2

Empty your seeds from their packages into small plastic kitchen bags for storage. Mark each one by putting the seed name on masking tape, then putting the tape on the bag. Pour the seeds into jar lids while you are working on the ornaments.

3 Draw a thin line with glue on the cardboard where the first row of seeds will be placed. On the bells, begin with the bottom row; on the hearts, begin with the outside row. Lay the seeds on top of the glue. Let the glue dry, then go on to the next row. Work on more than one ornament at a time. By the time you put one row of seeds on each ornament, the first one will be dry and ready for row 2.

■ Don't worry about getting glue on the top side of the seeds. The glue looks white when it is wet, but it will dry clear.

■ Pick out seeds for each ornament, watching for different colors, sizes, and shapes. You can look at our ornaments on *pages 110–111* for ideas.

■ You might find it easier to pick up seeds with tweezers. Smaller seeds may tend to stick to your fingers.

4 Add a second row of glue above the first row of seeds. Lay the second row of seeds in place and let the glue dry. Keep adding glue and seeds until you reach the top of the bell or the center of the heart. Some of the kitchen herbs and spices like sesame or dill seeds can be shaken out of the jar right onto the glue.

5 The bell ornament, *above*, uses squash seeds on the bottom, followed by sunflower, muskmelon, sesame, and more sunflower seeds, with a split pea at the top.

6 TO FINISH THE ORNAMENTS
The ornaments on *pages 110–111* have a gold cord edging with a loop at the top for hanging them on the Christmas tree. Cut a 16-inch piece of gold trim and fold it in half. Make a knot near the folded end so that you have a loop for hanging. Glue the loose ends of cord around the ornament, starting at the top and ending at the bottom. Trim off the ends of the cord so that they just meet each other.

From the top: Split pea, sunflower seeds, tapioca, sunflower seeds, hulled oats, and melon seeds

From the center: Sesame seeds, split peas, and sunflower seeds

This is a great project to make your imagination go to work for you. You'll find all the supplies you need in your garden and kitchen. Don't forget to check the spice rack for smaller things like sesame, poppy, or dill seeds. Cover large areas by sprinkling these small seeds onto glue-covered surfaces. Seeds that are long and narrow—like melon or sunflower seeds and hulled oats—make perfect edgings. On these two pages, we've given you examples of how different seeds will look when they're used on ornaments. You'll probably come up with beautiful designs of your own. Have fun.

From the top: Split pea, sunflower seeds, tapioca, apple seeds, split peas, sunflower seeds, and hulled oats

■ From the center: Tapioca, split peas, and hulled oats

■ From the top: Split pea, hulled oats, poppy and apple seeds, hulled oats, tapioca, oats, and melon seeds

■ From the top: Split pea; melon, sesame, and apple seeds; hulled oats; split peas; and melon seeds

■ From the center: Dill seeds, sunflower seeds, and hulled oats

■ From the center: Dill, apple, and melon seeds

LEAF PRINTS

It's fun to try printing with all kinds of leaves. Each leaf makes its own unique design. There are hundreds of trees and plants from which to pick nicely shaped leaves. Just be sure you ask permission before cutting leaves from houseplants, and if you gather leaves outdoors, don't come home with an armload of poison ivy.

GETTING STARTED

☐ Assorted leaves   ☐ Acrylic paint

☐ Newspapers   ☐ Artist's brushes

☐ Paper towels   ☐ Small roller

1 DOING THE PROJECT

Mix acrylic paints to get the color you want. Paint the side of the leaf where the veins feel raised. This is usually the back side.

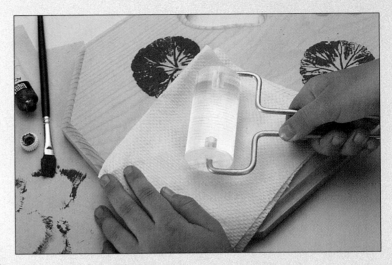

2 FINISHING THE PROJECT

Lay the leaf, painted side down, on wood or paper. Cover the leaf with paper towels and run a small roller over the paper.

3 Remove the paper towels and carefully lift up the leaf. You can probably make two prints before you add more paint. Let the paint dry thoroughly.

■ **Grape Ivy.** Pull apart leaf cluster and use only one section.

■ **Palm.** Use only one section from the leaf.

■ **Roses.** If you don't grow roses, ask a florist for a few leaves.

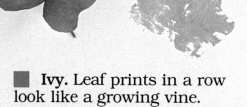

■ **Ivy.** Leaf prints in a row look like a growing vine.

■ **Hibiscus.** This plant has leaves that range from small to very large.

■ **New Guinea Impatiens.** Long, thin leaves for narrow projects.

■ **Coleus.** Has large veins.

■ **Chrysanthemum.** Shape fans out like branches on a tree.

■ **Beech Tree.** Tree leaves are best for bigger projects.

■ **Euonymus.** Press roller lightly on smooth leaves.

■ **Philodendron.** Always ask before taking leaves from houseplants.

■ **Geranium.** Don't worry about leaves that are curled. They flatten during the printing.

LEAF PROJECTS

Dad and Mom both will enjoy getting gifts to use when they are working in the garden. You can make leaf prints on glass, ceramics, clay pots, plastic, baskets, fabric, and many other materials.

Printed jars hold new seeds. A basket can be used to carry flowers or fresh tomatoes and other vegetables from the garden to the house. A colorful watering can, like the one *opposite*, keeps everything green and growing. A flowerpot printed with geranium leaves holds—you guessed it—a geranium.

THE FACES OF HALLOWEEN

The most important—and the most fun—
part of dressing up for Halloween is wearing
a mask so that no one will know
just who's playing tricks or begging for
treats. In this chapter, you'll find ways to
make some spectacular masks
so that even your closest friends and
neighbors won't recognize you!
The masks begin with the plain ones you can
buy in most stores right before Halloween,
and are jazzed up with all sorts of bright and
shiny materials. We also show you
crazy faces for your next jack-o'-lantern.

HALLOWEEN MASKS

On these two pages are the easy steps to make a black cat mask. Use the photograph on *pages 122–123* and the patterns on *pages 124–127* to make enough for you and all of your "spook" friends.

GETTING STARTED

- ☐ **Purchased mask**
- ☐ **¼-inch dowel:** 18 inches for each mask.
- ☐ **Crafts glue**
- ☐ **Felt**
- ☐ **Pipe cleaners**
- ☐ **Hot glue gun:** Ask for adult help.
- ☐ **Scissors**
- ☐ **Assorted trims**

1 DOING THE PROJECT
Find the pattern on *pages 124–127* for the mask you want to make. Cut out the shapes.

3 Look at the pictures of all the masks on *pages 122–123.* Use a strong crafts glue to attach all of the extra pieces, like the eyelashes and whiskers. Glue the glitter, sequins, ribbons, and silk flowers onto the mask.

4 **FINISHING THE PROJECT**
Ask an adult to help you attach the dowel using a hot glue gun. This will make a sturdy handle for holding onto the mask.

2 Buy the basic face mask at a dime store or theatrical shop. Glue the ears in place.

Adding the glitz. You can use any kind of glitter or trim that you like. The theatrical shops and fabric stores are full of fancy trims year-round. Be sure to use a strong crafts glue for attaching these decorations. A hot glue gun works very well, but can be dangerous to younger children because of the intense heat.

4

Attaching the handle. If you are right-handed, fasten the handle to the right side. If you are left-handed, glue the handle to the left side. The masks usually come with an elastic headband. Remove this band if you plan to add the handle.

5

HALLOWEEN MASKS

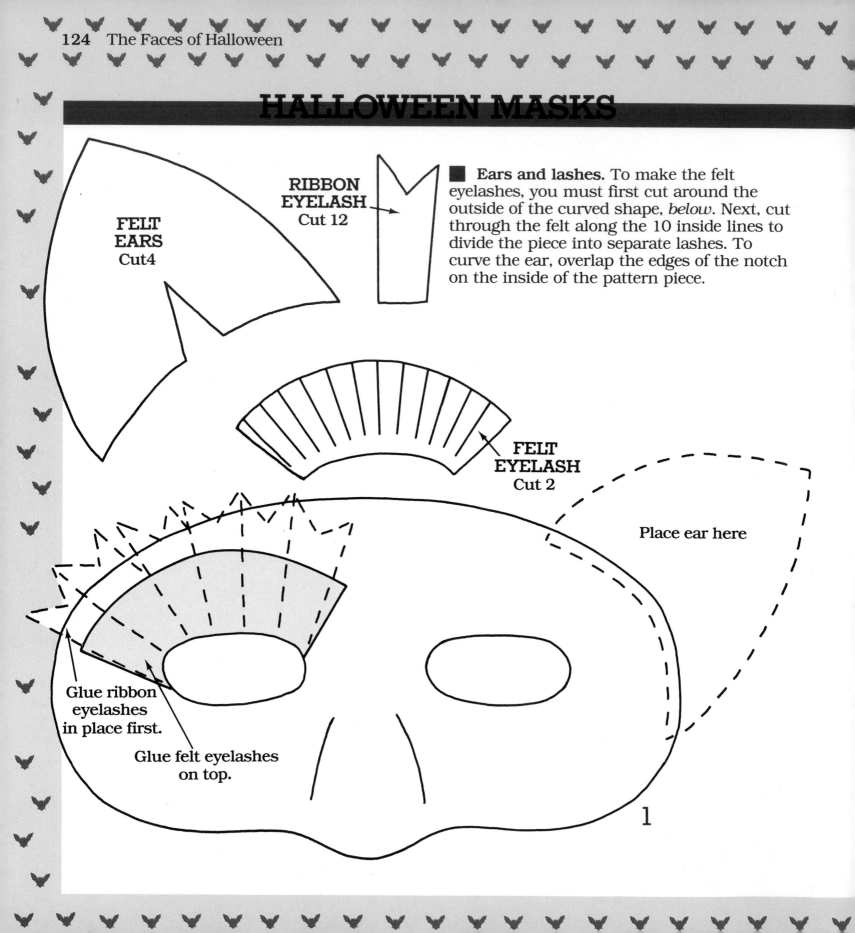

FELT EARS Cut 4

RIBBON EYELASH Cut 12

Ears and lashes. To make the felt eyelashes, you must first cut around the outside of the curved shape, *below*. Next, cut through the felt along the 10 inside lines to divide the piece into separate lashes. To curve the ear, overlap the edges of the notch on the inside of the pattern piece.

FELT EYELASH Cut 2

Place ear here

Glue ribbon eyelashes in place first.

Glue felt eyelashes on top.

1

Flowers, leaves, and ribbons. You may want to staple the thicker pieces like the flowers and leaves in place.

2

3

HALLOWEEN MASKS

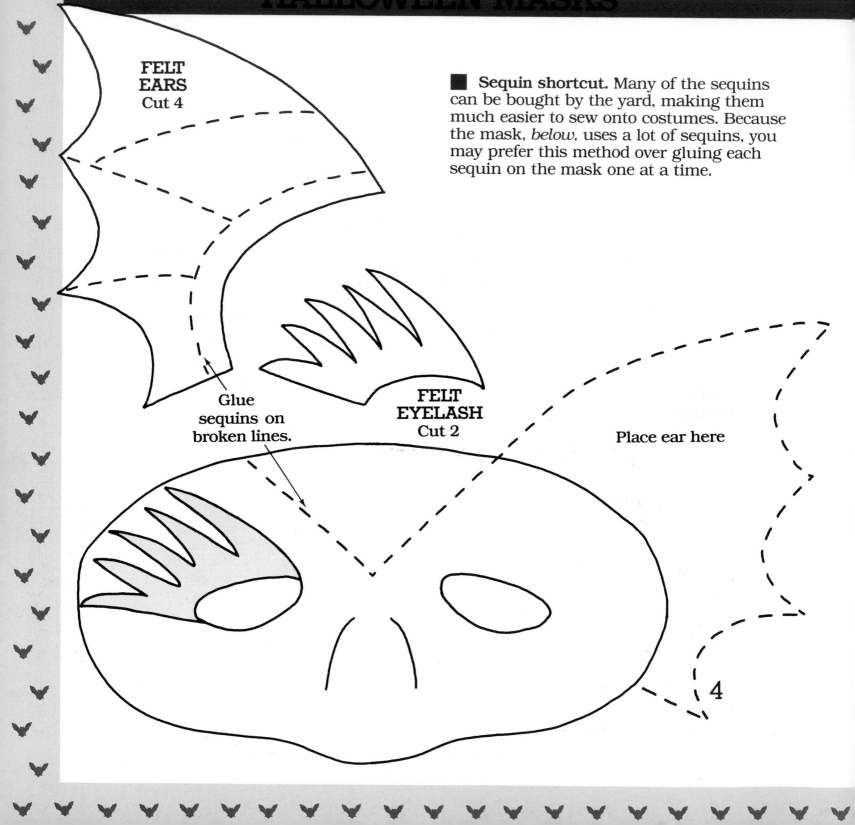

FELT EARS Cut 4

Sequin shortcut. Many of the sequins can be bought by the yard, making them much easier to sew onto costumes. Because the mask, *below,* uses a lot of sequins, you may prefer this method over gluing each sequin on the mask one at a time.

Glue sequins on broken lines.

FELT EYELASH Cut 2

Place ear here

4

Sharp edges. Any time you use feathers, larger sequins, or metal decorations, make very sure all sharp and pointed edges are trimmed and away from the eye area.

Ribbon cutting guide

5

PUMPKIN FACES

Cut out a section of pumpkin around the stem large enough to get your hand through. Remove the top. Use a spoon to scoop out everything inside of the pumpkin. Carve out the eyes, mouth, and other features, looking at the patterns on the following two pages for ideas. To make white teeth or eyes, cut through only the surface of the skin. Then use the knife to "peel" or cut back that layer. Make holes for ears and use pumpkin scraps with funny shapes to stick into those holes.

PUMPKIN FACES

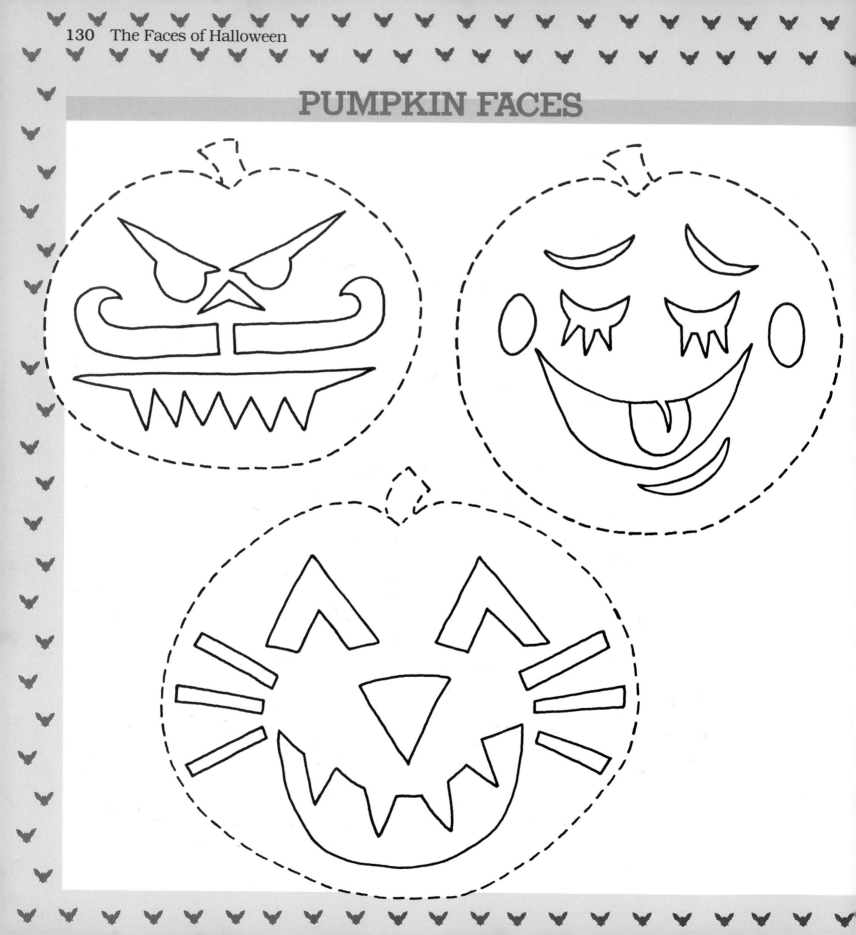

Halloween smiles. Carve your pumpkins using a variety of expressions on these pages, or make up some funny and scary faces of your own.

TABLETOP FUN FOR THANKSGIVING

A good way for you
to be a special part of Thanksgiving
dinner plans is to help decorate the table.
We've put together some great
ideas for you, including some Pilgrim place
mats (make them as a surprise for Mom and
Dad's places at the table), some name
cards made from pinecones and
Indian corn to set in front of each plate,
and a hilarious gaggle of "geese"
made from crookneck squash.

PILGRIM FACE MATS

To make the pattern for these 13-inch-tall face place mats, begin with the drawings on *pages 138–139*. You'll have to have an adult help you enlarge these to the right size.

GETTING STARTED

- ☐ **Felt:** Black, yellow, gray, blue, flesh, brown, white, and pink.
- ☐ **Transfer paper**
- ☐ **Pencil**
- ☐ **Scissors**
- ☐ **Yarn**
- ☐ **Crafts glue**

1 DOING THE PROJECT

Using the enlarged patterns from *pages 138–139*, outline pieces on felt using transfer paper. Cut out each shape.

2 FINISHING THE PROJECT

Lay the head shape faceup on a paper-covered work surface. Glue the hair pieces to the head along the dotted pattern lines. Glue the blue and black eye pieces to the face. Add the woman's pink cheeks and white hat. Glue the man's hatband to his hat and add the buckle. Glue the hat to the man's head. For the mouths, draw a thin line to form a smile. Glue or sew yarn along the line.

CORN PROJECTS

Before your Thanksgiving dinner, ask Mom how many people will be eating with you and make each one a napkin ring like the ones shown here. You can make place cards ahead of time and write the names on them while you're waiting for the turkey to get done.

GETTING STARTED

☐ White card stock
☐ Indian corn
☐ Cardboard tubes
☐ Crafts glue
☐ Pinecones
☐ Brown felt
☐ Press-on letters

■ **Making napkin rings.** Cut the cardboard tubes into 1-inch-wide sections—**ask an adult to help you** with this step. Cut felt into 1-inch-wide strips. Then cut the felt strip to fit *around* and *inside* the rings. Glue the felt in place. Let the glue dry. Dab the back of each kernel of Indian corn with glue. Place the corn kernels on the ring, lining them up in rows. Mix up the colors for a more interesting design.

JILL

■ **Making name cards.** Cut out each card using the pattern on *page 138.* Glue corn around the edges. Add the name with press-on letters. Tuck the cards into pinecones.

THANKSGIVING PROJECTS

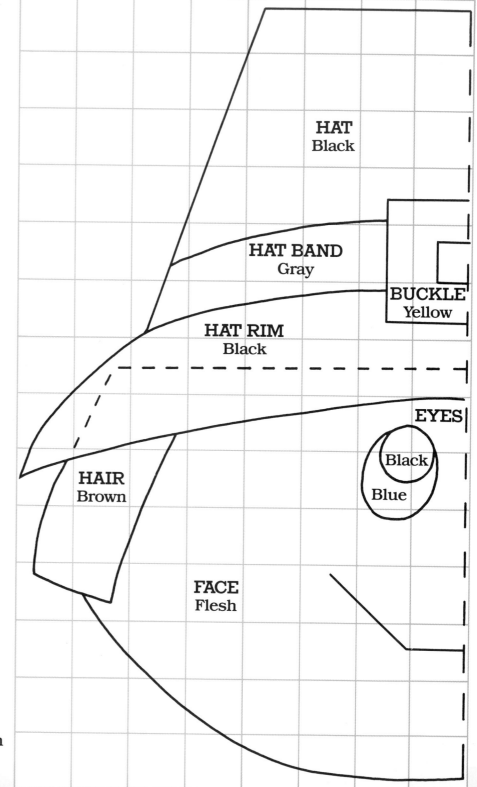

NAMECARD

HAT
Black

HAT BAND
Gray

BUCKLE
Yellow

HAT RIM
Black

EYES

Black

Blue

HAIR
Brown

FACE
Flesh

■ **Using these patterns:** The full-size pattern, *above,* is for the name cards shown on *pages 136–137.* Cut out this shape from white card stock for each guest.

The patterns, *right* and *opposite,* are for the Pilgrim Face Mats shown on *pages 134–135.* **Ask an adult to help you** enlarge the patterns to the right size.

1 Square = 1 Inch

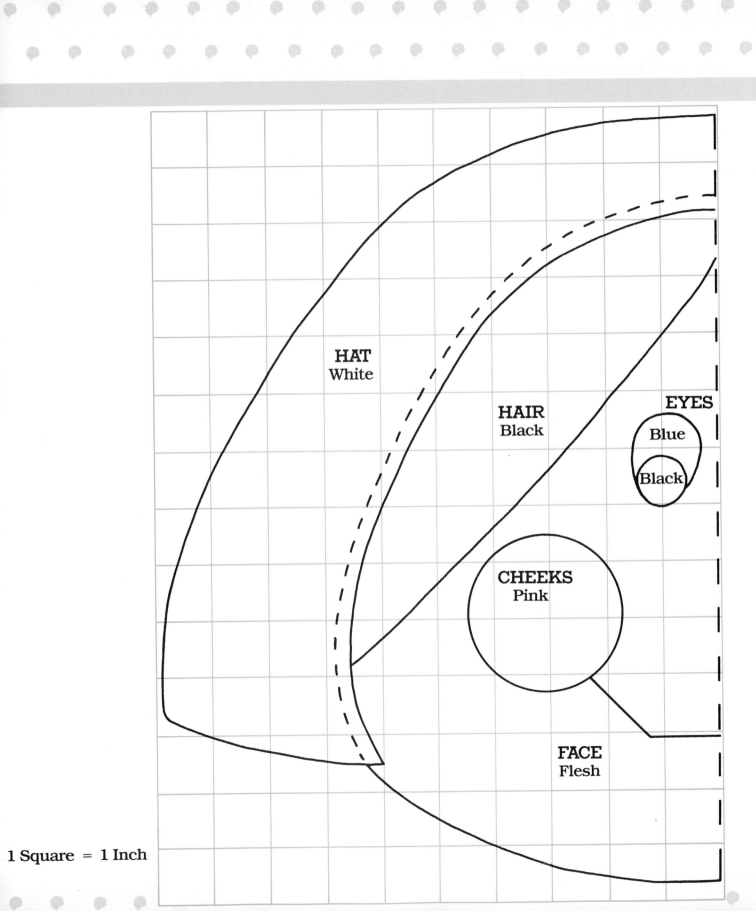

HAT
White

HAIR
Black

EYES
Blue
Black

CHEEKS
Pink

FACE
Flesh

1 Square = 1 Inch

A GAGGLE OF GEESE

Many fruits and vegetables grow into interesting shapes. A certain kind of summer squash grows with a long, thin "neck" that forms a curve. You can make some funny geese like the ones, *opposite*, by just adding some clove eyes to the "heads" of the squash.

GETTING STARTED

- ☐ **Crookneck squash:** Find some with part of the stems attached—the stems form the beaks.

- ☐ **Sharp knife**

- ☐ **Cutting board**

- ☐ **Waxed paper or cardboard**

- ☐ **Ice pick or awl**

- ☐ **Whole cloves**

- ☐ **Dried leaves**

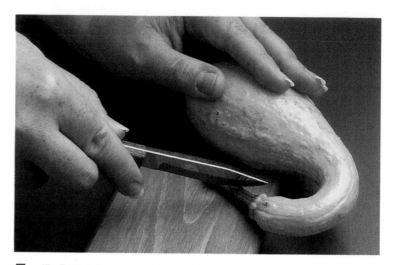

1 DOING THE PROJECT

Wash any dirt off the squash and dry it with a paper towel. **Ask an adult to help** cut the stem of the squash at an angle to make it look like a beak. Use an ice pick or awl to make two small holes in each goose's "face." Insert a whole clove into each hole to make the eyes.

2 FINISHING THE PROJECT

Slice off the large rounded end of the squash so that it will stand upright without tipping over. The squash does have enough natural moisture to damage a wooden surface, so you must set the cut end on a piece of waxed paper or cardboard.

STAR-SPANGLED CHRISTMAS

You might not be able
to count all the stars in the sky, but
you can probably count the stars on your
next Christmas tree. Our Christmas
ornaments and decorations that
you can make have some unusual stars
that will make your Christmas tree
glow—from bright and shiny stars made
from glitter and glue to paper ones
with funny faces. We've also included a
treetop angel you can cut out from
a couple of white paper plates.

GLITTER STARS

Here's one of the simplest holiday trims you can make...and one of the most exciting for any person at any age. In just a few minutes, you can turn out dozens of stars for Christmas or Fourth of July decorating.

GETTING STARTED

- ☐ Glitter in assorted colors
- ☐ Waxed paper
- ☐ White crafts glue: Select one that dries hard.

1 DOING THE PROJECT

Use a bottle of glue with a pointed tip to "draw" a star shape on waxed paper. Don't try to make the star shapes too perfect.

2 FINISHING THE PROJECT

Sprinkle the glue with glitter. Make sure it is completely covered. Let the stars dry for 48 hours. Carefully peel the waxed paper away from the back, working in from each point.

STAR FACES

You can make these wonderful Christmas characters by the bunch to tie onto wreaths and packages, or to decorate the tree. Use a special shiny-surface paper from the art store, like the paper we've used here, or substitute construction paper for a no-shine finish. Any medium-weight paper works.

Full-size patterns for the star faces appear on *pages 150–151.*

GETTING STARTED

☐ Artist's Color Cast paper (or use construction paper)

☐ Tissue paper

☐ Pencil

☐ Scissors

☐ White crafts glue

☐ Paper punch

☐ Cotton balls

☐ Hammer

☐ Nail

☐ Brads

☐ Ribbon

☐ Masking tape

☐ Pipe cleaner

DOING THE PROJECT

Use the pictures on *pages 148–149* for colors and the patterns on *pages 150–151.* Trace the pattern pieces onto tracing paper.

Lay the pattern pieces facedown on paper and cut out the shapes for the Santa. Glue the head and hat to the star.

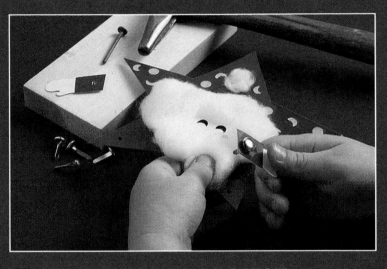

To make a moon shape, first punch a full circle with your paper punch. Then, punch part of a circle, using one side of the hole you have just made for the inside of the moon.

FINISHING THE PROJECT
Glue the hand to the arm. Pound a nail through both pieces where they will join. Push a brad through the hole. Open the prongs at the back of the star to hold the brad in place.

Glue moon eyes and circle cheeks to the face. Add other circles and moons to the star just for fun. Decorate the hat with cotton and add a cotton-ball beard.

GIRL WITH CURLS

For this star you use the face, hat, and arm shapes that you used for Santa, *pages 146–147.* Glue the face to the star. Cut paper ribbon into 3-inch lengths. Use the sharp edge of your scissors to curl the ribbon. Tuck the curls under the hat as you glue it into place. Add a cotton top to the hat; add circles, hearts, and moons to the face and star background. Glue the cuff to the hand shape. Attach the arms to the star with brads, just like you did for Santa on *page 147.*

POLKA DOT REINDEER

Rudolph's red nose probably doesn't shine any brighter than the reindeer star ornament, *above.* This reindeer's antlers are full of colorful lights to lead the way on Christmas morning. Cut out pointed paper antler shapes and glue them on the top of the head in every possible direction. Punch out lots of colored circles and glue them in place to jazz up this well-known holiday character. (Patterns are on *pages 150–151.*)

JACK-IN-THE-BOX

This funny little guy is sure to surprise anybody. Use the pattern on *pages 150–151* for the "box" and the man. Start by gluing the box to the star. Twist a pipe cleaner into a coil or spring shape that measures about 1 inch across. Tuck one end under the box flap and glue it in place. Glue the hat to Jack's head, and the head to the body. Add arms, cotton hair, and facial features. Glue the second end of the pipe cleaner to the back of Jack's body.

SMILING SNOWMAN

Use the patterns on *pages 150–151*. Cut out the face of our happy snowman and glue it to the star. Give him a black top hat trimmed in Christmas holly. Make a two-toned scarf by first cutting the bottom color in one pattern piece. Then use your pattern to cut out the striped pieces in a second color. Glue the stripes in place on the scarf. Attach the hand and arm pieces to the star just like you did for the Santa star on *page 147*.

STAR FACE PATTERNS

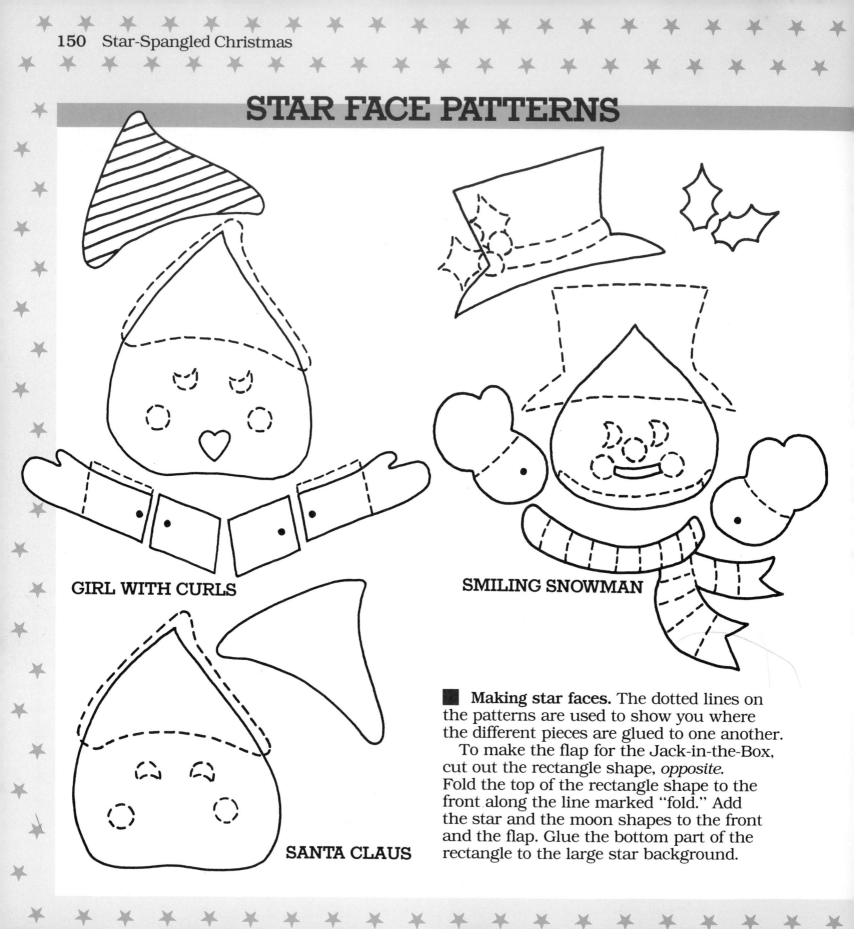

GIRL WITH CURLS

SANTA CLAUS

SMILING SNOWMAN

■ **Making star faces.** The dotted lines on the patterns are used to show you where the different pieces are glued to one another.

To make the flap for the Jack-in-the-Box, cut out the rectangle shape, *opposite.* Fold the top of the rectangle shape to the front along the line marked "fold." Add the star and the moon shapes to the front and the flap. Glue the bottom part of the rectangle to the large star background.

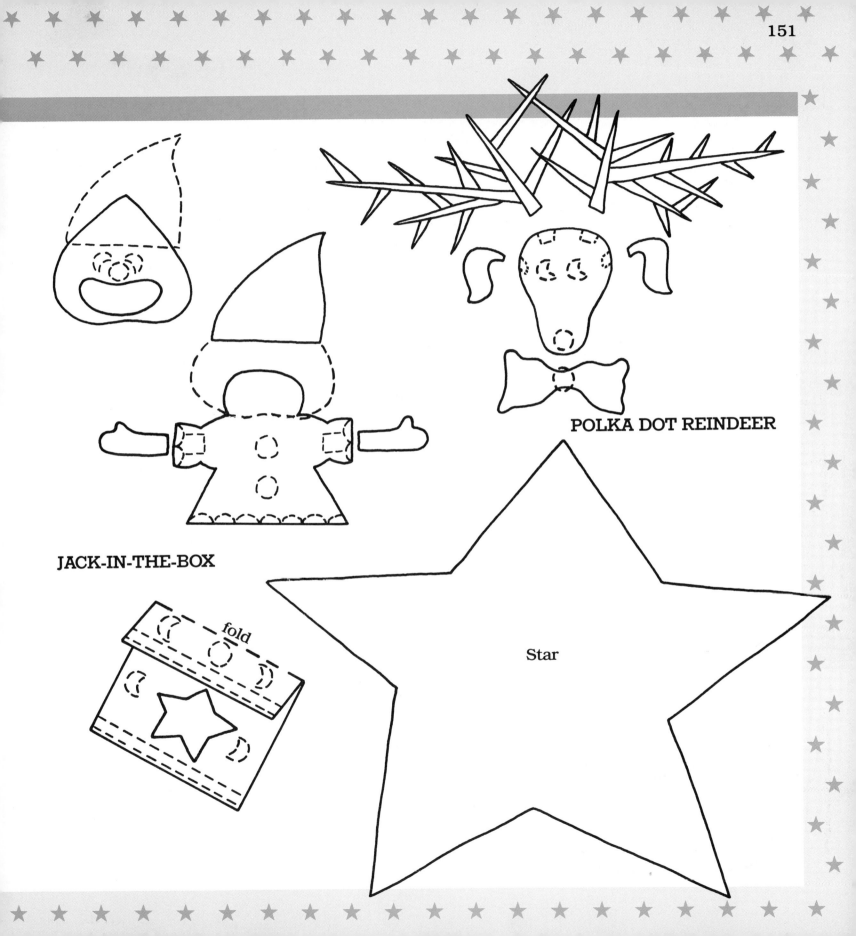

POLKA DOT REINDEER

JACK-IN-THE-BOX

fold

Star

PAPER-PLATE ANGELS

The heavenly angels pictured here are easy to make from paper plates. You'll want to make lots of them—one for the treetop, some to sit in among the evergreen branches and on top of Christmas packages, and more for the windowsills or holiday table decorations. A simple pattern for making the angels follows on *pages 154–155* with folding instructions on *pages 156–157.*

GETTING STARTED

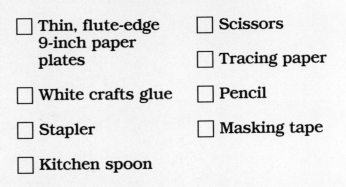

☐ Thin, flute-edge 9-inch paper plates

☐ White crafts glue

☐ Stapler

☐ Kitchen spoon

☐ Scissors

☐ Tracing paper

☐ Pencil

☐ Masking tape

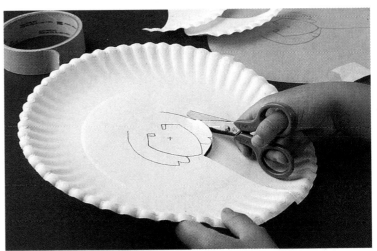

1 DOING THE PROJECT
Here is an easy way to transfer patterns to paper. Use a soft pencil to trace the pattern on *pages 154–155* onto tissue paper. Center the tissue with the pencil markings facedown on the paper plate. Stick it in place on the plate with small pieces of masking tape. Use the back side of a spoon to rub over the pencil lines. This will cause the pencil drawing to rub off onto the plate. Rub only the "slit" line and the head lines. The outside circle is given only to help you center the design on the plate.

2 Transfer the left and right wing patterns in the same way. The pattern shows you where to place the edge of the wing so that the scallops of the plate become the ruffles on the edge of the angel's wings.

Cut the line marked "slit" from the edge of the plate up to the head. Use small scissors to cut all solid lines. In the head area you will see two small rectangles. Cut them out. These cutouts form the bottom shape of the hair. (See *page 154.*) Do not cut the two dotted lines. We will explain these later.

PAPER-PLATE ANGELS

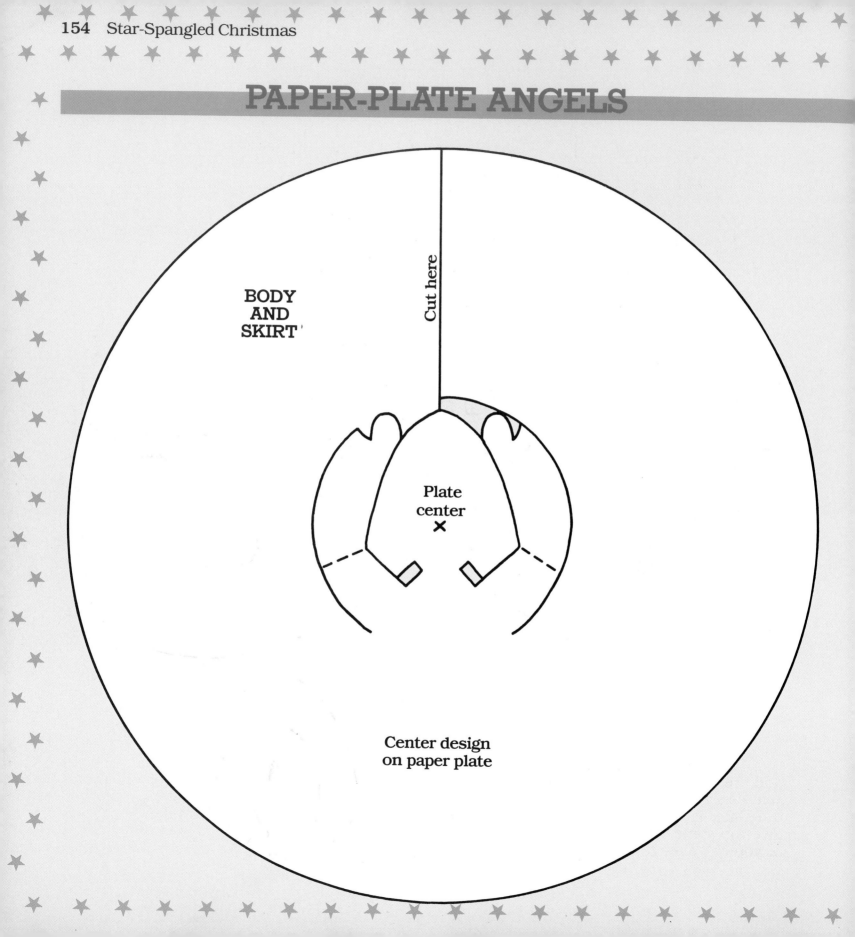

BODY
AND
SKIRT

Cut here

Plate
center
✕

Center design
on paper plate

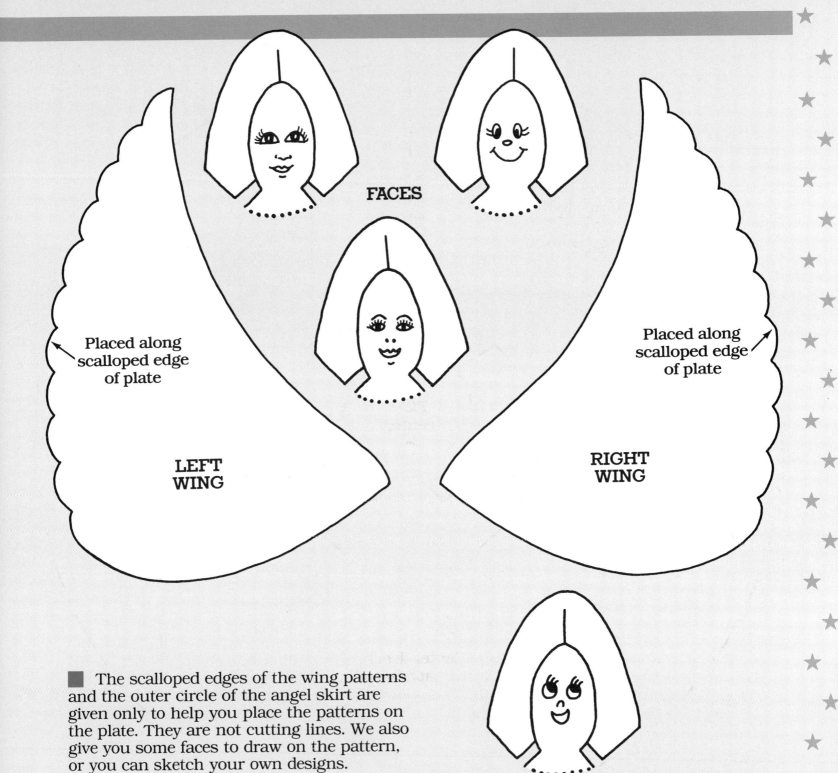

FACES

Placed along
scalloped edge
of plate

Placed along
scalloped edge
of plate

LEFT
WING

RIGHT
WING

■ The scalloped edges of the wing patterns
and the outer circle of the angel skirt are
given only to help you place the patterns on
the plate. They are not cutting lines. We also
give you some faces to draw on the pattern,
or you can sketch your own designs.

PAPER-PLATE ANGELS

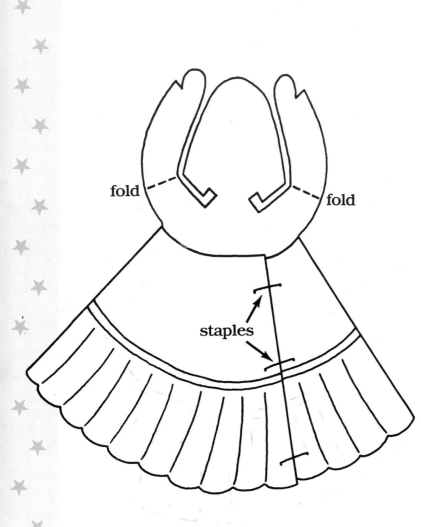

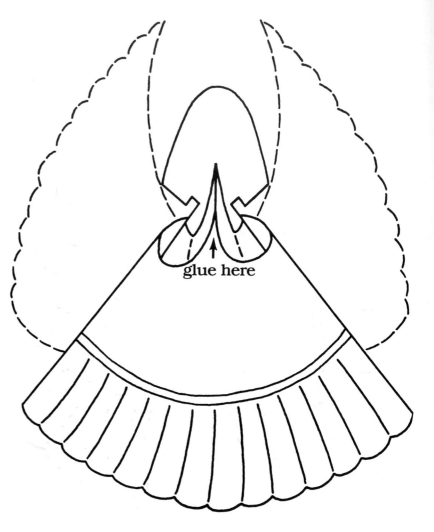

1 SHAPING THE SKIRT

Turn the plate over so the edge curves to the inside and all the pencil marks are to the back side. Hold the two skirt edges where you cut the "slit" and overlap them about 3 inches. Staple the edges together to hold the skirt in place. (See the drawing, *above*.)

2 MAKING PRAYING HANDS

Pull the hands and head forward slightly. Bend the arms away from the body. Bend them again at the elbow so that the tips of the fingers touch in a praying position. Add a dot of crafts glue to the fingertips (see the drawing, *above*) and press them together. Let the glue dry.

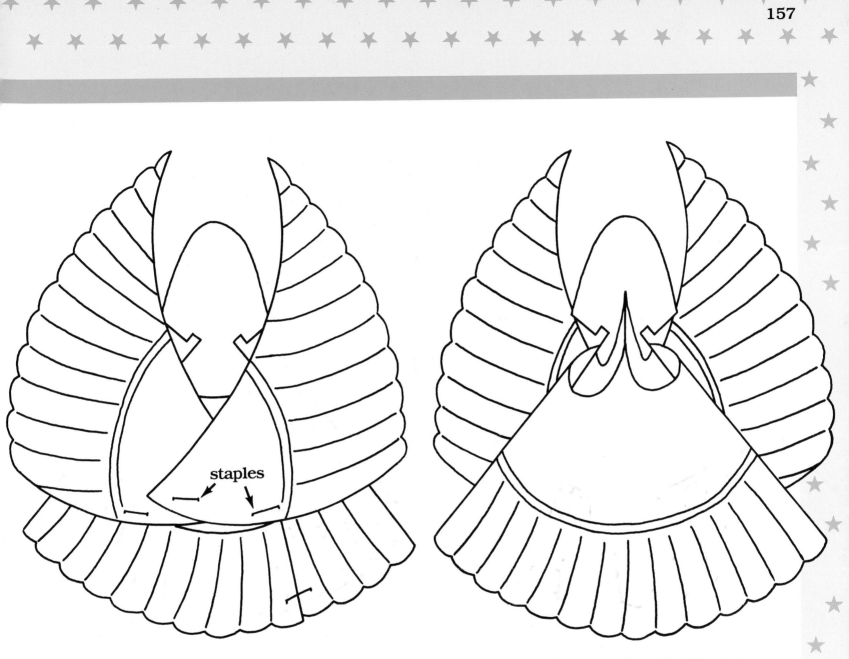

staples

3 ADDING THE WINGS

Use your hands to curve the paper wings slightly so that they roll toward the back, away from the angel's body. Staple them in place, one on top of the other, onto the back of the angel's skirt. (The drawing, *above*, will help you decide where to place the staples.)

4 FINISHING THE PROJECT

You can give each angel a smiling face using the designs on *page 155*, or make up some of your own. Use light-color pencils or pastel-color crayons. You also may want to decorate the skirts with ribbons, stars, glitter, or stickers. Use your imagination for hours of fun.

CHRISTMAS PATTERN PORTFOLIO

In this holiday pattern section, we have given you a choice of shapes to use when you design your own gifts, cards, gift wrap, ornaments, and more. There will be something here for almost everyone. Use your imagination for hours of crafting enjoyment.

CHRISTMAS PATTERN PORTFOLIO

CHRISTMAS PATTERN PORTFOLIO

CHRISTMAS PATTERN PORTFOLIO

JULY WEEKEND CELEBRATIONS

The Fourth of July is the day we
celebrate the birthday of our country. And in
the summertime, it's the most fun to
get together with family and friends on a
picnic. To make your picnic complete,
craft a special tablecloth and a barbecue
apron, and decorate a picnic basket to match.
We show some tablecloths made
from vinyl so that even the rain won't hurt
them, and other fabric accessories
that are decorated with your own artwork.

4TH OF JULY PICNIC

Getting decorations and games ready for a special picnic is almost as much fun as the picnic itself! The tablecloths shown on *pages 166–167* are perfect for the Fourth of July. You can make them quickly with adhesive-backed vinyl that comes in lots of bright colors.

GETTING STARTED

- [ ] **Vinyl or oilcloth:** Cut it in 36-inch squares.

- [ ] **Scissors**

- [ ] **Transfer paper**

- [ ] **Pencil**

- [ ] **Adhesive-backed vinyl:** Red, black, flesh, white, blue, and yellow (plus silver for the firecracker tablecloth).

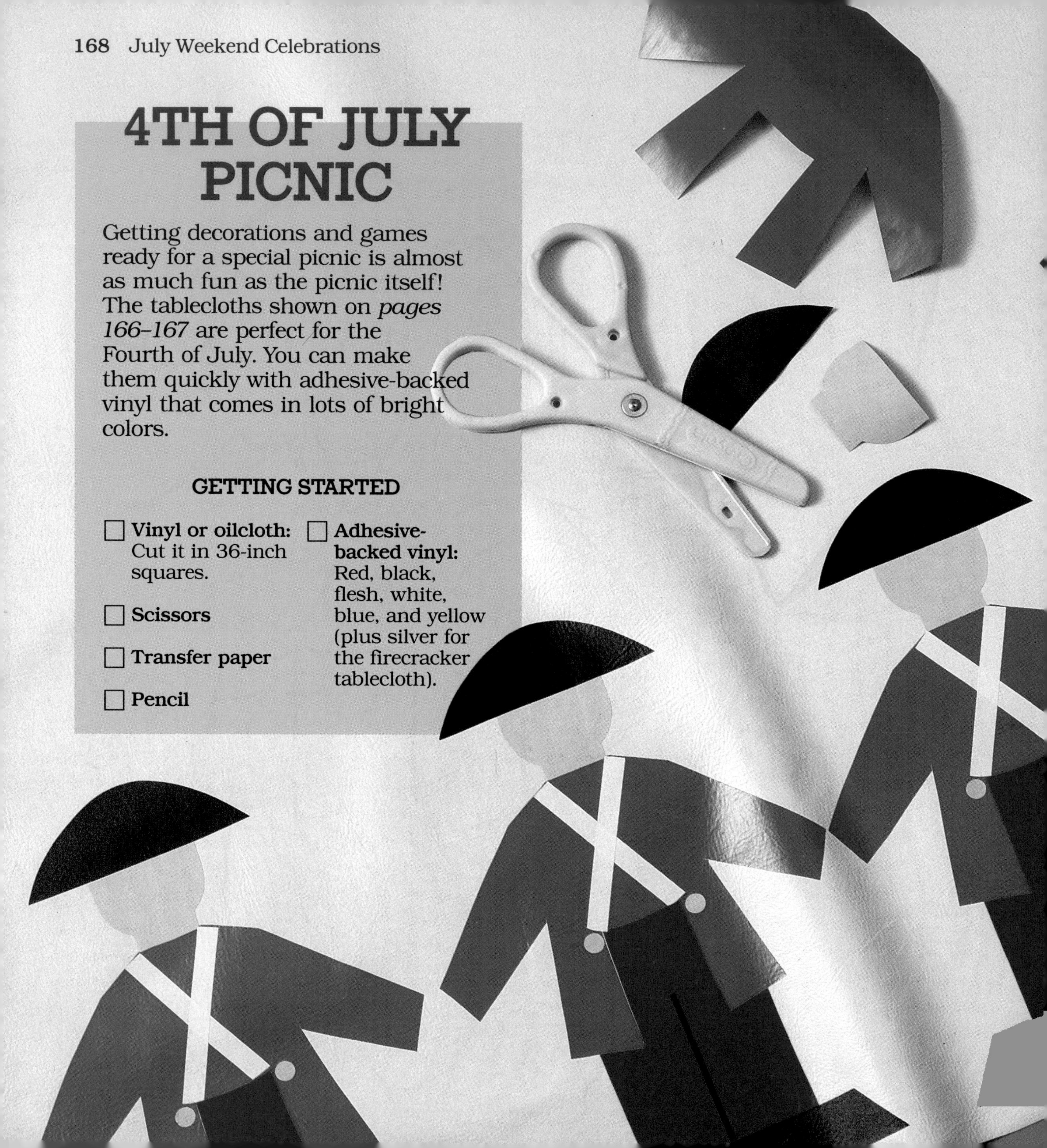

1 DOING THE PROJECT

Use the full-size patterns on *pages 170–171* for the Soldiers Tablecloth and cut out enough shapes from adhesive-backed vinyl for 16 soldiers. Cut out 12 red vinyl stars. Using the full-size patterns on *pages 172–173* for the Firecracker Tablecloth, cut out 10 stars, and shapes for four firecrackers, four flares, and two explosions.

2

Following the position diagrams given for both tablecloths (*page 171* and *page 172*), place the shapes on the tablecloth. Peel the backing paper off each shape and press it down firmly on the vinyl background.

SOLDIERS TABLECLOTH

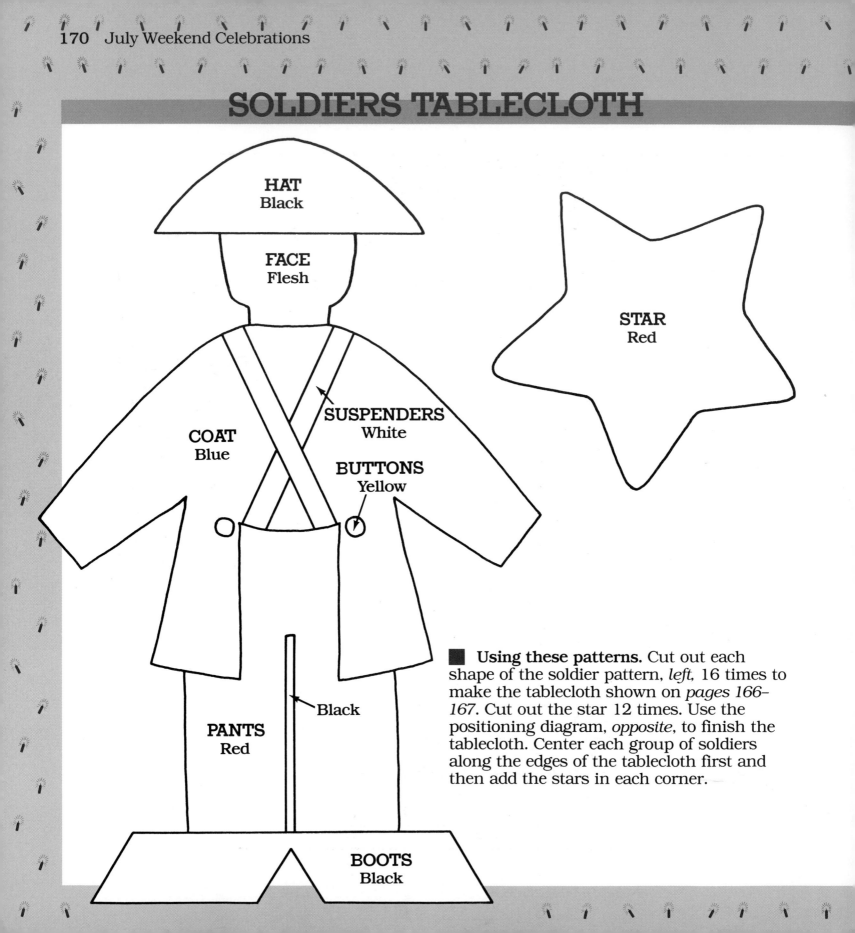

HAT
Black

FACE
Flesh

STAR
Red

SUSPENDERS
White

COAT
Blue

BUTTONS
Yellow

Black

PANTS
Red

BOOTS
Black

■ **Using these patterns.** Cut out each shape of the soldier pattern, *left,* 16 times to make the tablecloth shown on *pages 166–167.* Cut out the star 12 times. Use the positioning diagram, *opposite,* to finish the tablecloth. Center each group of soldiers along the edges of the tablecloth first and then add the stars in each corner.

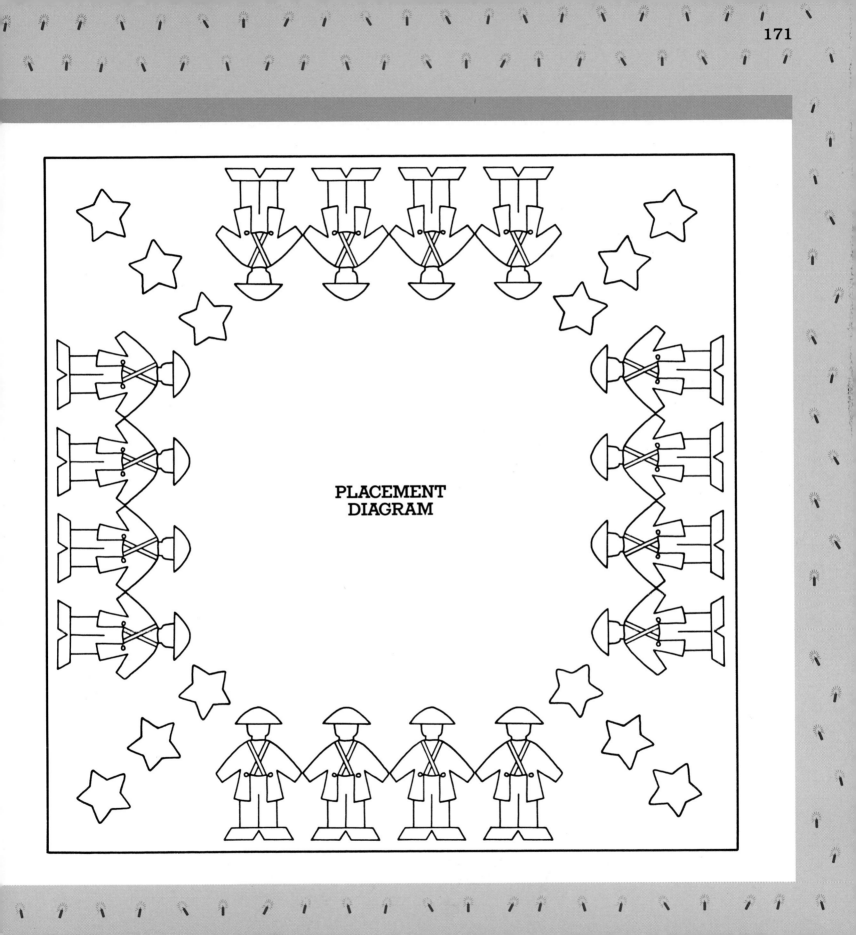

PLACEMENT
DIAGRAM

FIRECRACKER TABLECLOTH

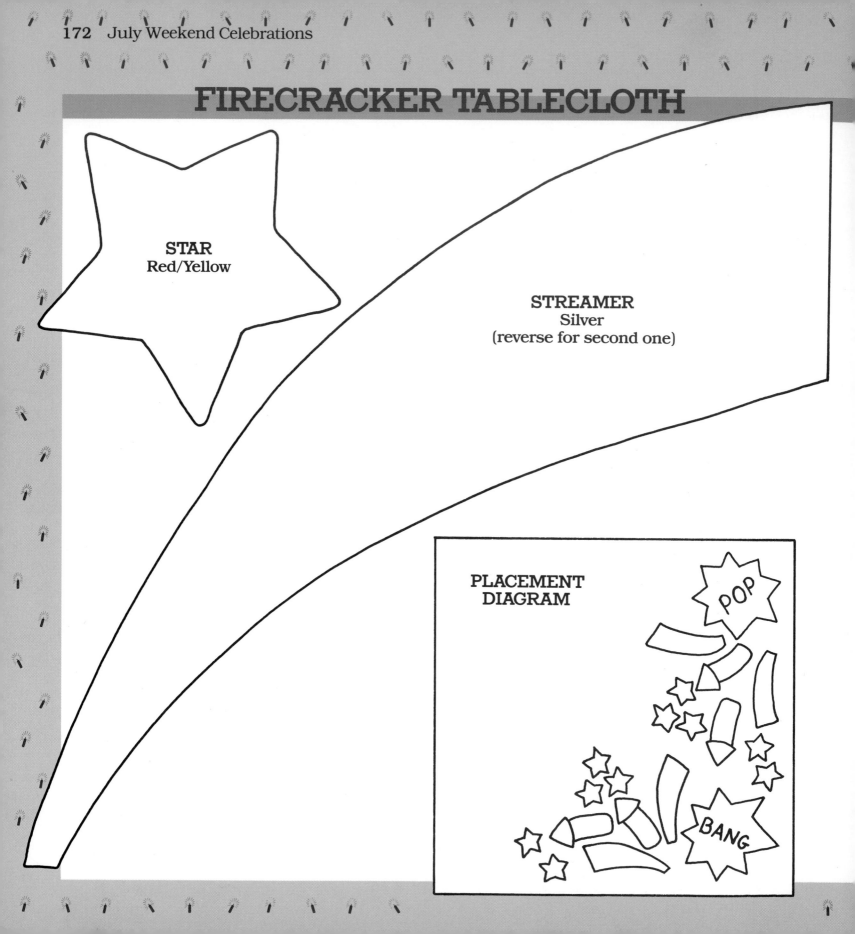

STAR
Red/Yellow

STREAMER
Silver
(reverse for second one)

**PLACEMENT
DIAGRAM**

POP

BANG

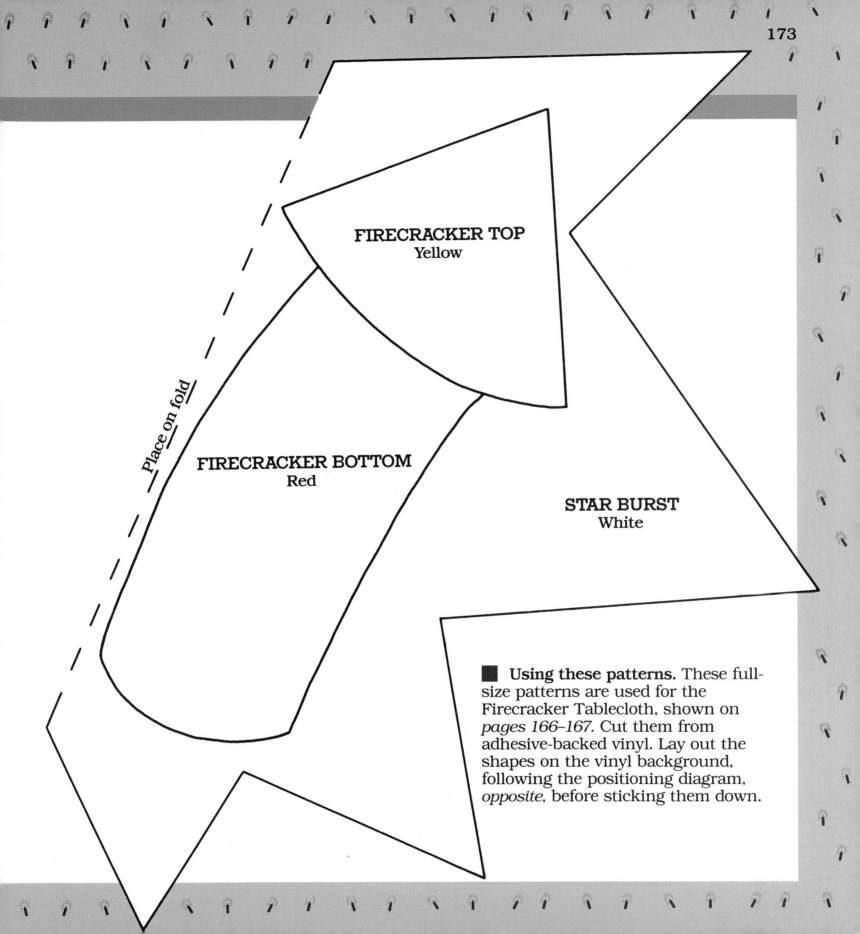

FIRECRACKER TOP
Yellow

Place on fold

FIRECRACKER BOTTOM
Red

STAR BURST
White

Using these patterns. These full-size patterns are used for the Firecracker Tablecloth, shown on *pages 166–167.* Cut them from adhesive-backed vinyl. Lay out the shapes on the vinyl background, following the positioning diagram, *opposite,* before sticking them down.

COLORING PROJECTS

The crayons used for making the projects on *pages 176–177* are different from ordinary crayons. Any design you draw with these crayons can be transferred to fabric by using an iron. Be sure that you have an adult help you when you begin the transfer step.

GETTING STARTED

☐ Watercolor paper

☐ Fabric transfer crayons

☐ Permanent felt-tip markers

☐ Iron

☐ Dish towels

☐ Tablecloths

☐ Napkins

☐ Apron

1 DOING THE PROJECT

Remember that every picture you color with the fabric transfer crayons will end up printing backward!

BBQ APRON

To make an apron like the one, *below,* find an apron with a light-color front. (You can buy these ready-made or have someone make one for you using a pattern from the fabric store.) For best results with all of the fabric transfer crayon projects, look for items that are labeled "Cotton/Polyester" blend.

Cut a piece of paper to fit across the front of the apron, and color a picture on it. A picture of food that's barbecued or a drawing of someone you know cooking at a grill would be perfect for an apron design.

Have an adult transfer the drawing to the apron with an iron, following the directions on the crayon package.

NAPKINS

■ Smaller projects like the napkins, *above,* are good to experiment with before making a whole tablecloth. Use cloth napkins, or have someone who sews hem squares of light-color fabric. Outline some shapes or add names or words with a permanent marker.

TABLECLOTH AND TEA TOWELS

■ **Making the tablecloth.** This is a good project for a group of kids to work on because it takes so many drawings to cover a large area. You might want to make all of the drawings relate to a topic, such as a day at the zoo or a trip to a carnival. When all the drawings are done, decide where they should go and **have an adult transfer them** with an iron.

■ **Making tea towels.** Tea towels make good presents for Grandma and Grandpa. Remember that drawings end up printing backward on the fabric, and that you'll need to add greetings and your name with a permanent marker **after** the drawings are transferred to the towels.

QUICK-AS-A-WINK
CARDS & WRAPS

You can add your own
personal touch to store-bought gifts
by making the paper to wrap them in.
Or, attach a card
that you've created especially for the occasion.
This chapter has some great ideas,
and they're fun to do. Some of the ways we've
decorated the paper might get a bit messy,
so be sure to work outdoors or
in an area that's easy for you to clean up.

STAMP-PAD PRINTS

Making the stamps from bottle corks will require help from an adult. The crafts knife has a very sharp cutting blade and could be dangerous for smaller hands to use.

But, the printing is easy and loads of fun. You won't need any help to stamp beautiful wrapping paper and cards for your Christmas presents.

GETTING STARTED

- ☐ **Assorted bottle corks**
- ☐ **Crafts knife:** Ask for adult help, please.
- ☐ **White kraft paper**
- ☐ **Stamp pads in assorted colors**
- ☐ **Newspapers**
- ☐ **Pencil**

1 DOING THE PROJECT
Pick up a supply of corks at a store that sells wine-making supplies, or have someone save them for you. Use a pencil to draw your pattern on the bigger end of the cork. **Ask an adult** to cut away the edge of the cork with a crafts knife, leaving only the shape you have drawn. (See the photograph, *above*, and the patterns on *page 165.*) Cut the cork away at least ¼ inch deeper than the surface.

2 Buy pre-inked stamp pads in a bunch of bright colors. You also can buy ink in bottles to resoak the pads as they begin to dry. **Wear old clothes** in case you get any ink on yourself. Ink does not always wash out.

3 FINISHING THE PROJECT
Spread out white kraft paper over newspaper or scrap paper. Press the cork onto the ink pad and then transfer it to the white paper. (See the photograph, *above*.) Let it dry, then wrap up your Christmas surprises.

SPLATTER PAINTING

If you can shake your wrist, you can make these great wrapping papers for all of the holidays. On these two pages, we've shown you how to make the gift wrap using white paper and colored paint. Be sure to try using white paint and brightly colored papers for a different look.

GETTING STARTED

☐ **White kraft paper:** Available at art stores.

☐ **Tempera paints**

☐ **Eyedroppers:** Available at the drugstore.

☐ **Newspapers or brown butcher paper**

☐ **Small bowls or lids**

2 Pour a little bit of paint into a small bowl or jar lid. You will need one lid for each color. To fill the dropper, first squeeze the air out of the bulb. Then put the clear glass end into the paint and stop squeezing the bulb. Paint will fill the dropper.

1 DOING THE PROJECT

Ask an adult to take you to the local drugstore to buy eyedroppers. Pick up at least one eyedropper for each color of paint you plan to use on your gift wrap. The white kraft paper that we used comes in big rolls and can be bought by the yard at the art store.

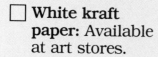 This project can be very messy. Wear your oldest clothes. Find a place to work that will make you and your parents happy. The basement or garage floor may be just right. Cover your work space with old newspapers. Lay the white kraft paper on top of the newspapers.

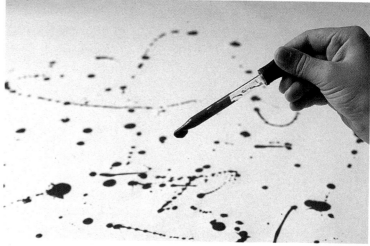

3 FINISHING THE PROJECT

To make paint spots, hold the dropper over the paper. Bring your wrist up slowly. Then, using a quick and firm motion, shake the dropper down toward the paper. Paint will spill out in drops each time you shake the dropper. (Don't squeeze the bulb or all of the paint will come out at once.) Let the paint dry completely.

TOOTHBRUSH PAINTING

Make your own Christmas cards this year using paint, paper, and your old toothbrushes. Be sure to send a card to your dentist.

Use our full-size patterns on *page 188*, or make up some of your own.

GETTING STARTED

☐ **Construction paper**

☐ **Acrylic paints**

☐ **Tracing paper**

☐ **Old toothbrushes:** One for each paint color.

☐ **Pen or pencil**

☐ **Scissors**

☐ **Newspaper or brown kraft paper**

1 DOING THE PROJECT

Trace the patterns on *page 188* onto paper. Cut out the shapes. Fold one 8½x11-inch piece of construction paper in half widthwise for each card. Lay the card on kraft paper or newspaper.

2 FINISHING THE PROJECT

Lay the pattern on top of the card. Dip the toothbrush into the paint. Tap the brush on the edge of the paint jar to get rid of the extra paint that would drip onto the paper. Hold the brush over the card with one hand. Run the "pointer" finger of your other hand through the bristles. Splatter all of the area not covered by the pattern. Let the paint dry before you try to pick the pattern piece off the card.

CUTTING SHAPES

Make paper chains of snowmen, Christmas trees, Santas, and more. Tape them around packages, hook bunches of them together to loop around the tree, or use them to decorate the fireplace or wall.

Use the full-size patterns on *page 189* for hours of scissor-happy entertainment.

GETTING STARTED

☐ **Lightweight white paper:** Use watercolor, kraft, construction, and other papers from the art or crafts store.

☐ Tracing paper

☐ Pen or pencil

☐ Scissors

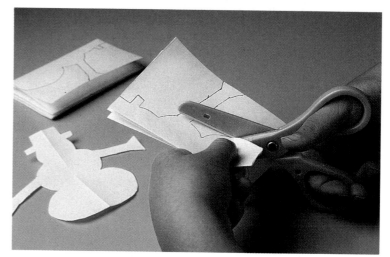

1 DOING THE PROJECT

Use tracing paper and a pen or pencil to copy the patterns on *page 189*. Cut white paper into long strips that are 4 inches deep.

■ **Cutting the paper.** Fold the first piece of the paper strip so that it is 2½ inches wide. Then continue folding the strip accordion- or fan-style. See the photograph, *above*.

2 FINISHING THE PROJECT

Lay the pattern on top of the folded paper strip and trace the shape onto the top section of the paper. Cut out the shape through all layers of the paper. Open up the folded paper and see the row of identical shapes you have made with just a few simple scissors cuts.

PAPER CUTTING AND PAINTING

ACKNOWLEDGMENTS

DESIGNERS

We wish to express our appreciation to the talented people who created the designs and projects for this book.

Chris Noah-Cooper—pierced paper, 76, 78–81
Heather Cravens—paper collage valentines, 38, 40–41
Phyllis Dunstan—candy-filled hearts, 42–43; place mats, napkin rings, place cards, 132, 134–137; tablecloths, 166, 168–169; cork printing, 180–181
Martha Ehrlich—star faces, 142, 145–149
Linda Emmerson—vegetable prints, 86–93
Kathy Engel—pumpkins 118, 128–129
Dixie Falls—cross-stitched pincushion, 44–45
Nina Gordon—dough projects, 22, 24–37
Stacey Molloy—painted ornaments, 18–19
Ellen Morello—gift wrap, 183
Bev Rivers—roll-ups, 68–69; leaf prints, 112–117; glitter stars, 142, 144–145
Carole Rodgers—flower press, flower gifts, 96–105
Mimi Shimmin—Halloween masks, 118, 120–123
Rachel and Ryan Sindelar—crayon transfers, 174–175
Barbara Smith—angels, 142, 152–153
Polly Thornton—wreaths, 8–13
Sara Jane Treinen—cut-paper heart, 48–49
Jim Williams—paper bunny, 46–47; wall border, 178

Mavis Wilson—geese centerpiece, 132, 140–141
Ed Wong—spattered gift wrap, 184–185; cut paper, 186–187
Pamela Woods—seed ornaments, 108–111

PHOTOGRAPHERS

A special thanks to the photographers whose creative talents and technical skills contributed to the book's production.

Mike Dieter—cover, 23, 44, 46–47, 77, 143, 179

Hedrich-Blessing—183

Hopkins Associates—17–19, 24–31, 34, 37, 40–43, 68–73, 76, 78–81, 86–87, 91, 92–93, 114–115, 120–123, 128–129, 134–137, 140–141, 168–169, 174–177, 178, 180–187

Scott Little—152

Perry Struse—6, 8–16, 22, 38, 44–45, 48–49, 66, 88–90, 94, 96–105, 108–113, 116–117, 118, 132, 142, 144–147, 166

SPECIAL THANKS

To the children who proved that the projects are fun to do.

Abbie, A'Leisha, Amy, Bea, Brenda, Floyd, Heidi, Jacob, Jeff, Johnny, Justin, Kathy, Kevin, Kirsten, Kristin, Lacy, Lindsay, Luke, Mark, Mary Delaney, Megan, Molly, Rachel, Ryan, and Valerie.

Thanks to those folks who so generously shared their time and materials with us.

Barbara Bergman

Gary Boling

Jerry Brown

C.M. Offray and Son, Inc.
261 Madison Ave.
New York, NY 10016

DMC
107 Trumbull St.
Elizabeth, NJ 07206

Dot's Frame Shop
4717 Fleur Dr.
Des Moines, IA 50321

Barb and Sue Forbes

Patricia Heggen

The Horchow Collection
Box 650098
Dallas, TX 75265-0098

Jean Logan

Margaret Sindelar

V-7 Produce
4385 NE. 54th Ave.
Des Moines, IA 50317

Roger Vriezelaar

Wine World-Corks
419 Washington St.
Cedar Falls, IA 50613

INDEX

INDEX